THE WORLD RUNS ON RUBBER

THE WORLD RUNS ON RUBBER

THE STORY OF KAL TIRE

Library and Archives Canada Cataloguing in Publication

Lilley, Wayne, 1943—
    The world runs on rubber : the story of Kal Tire / Wayne Lilley.

ISBN 978-0-9866361-3-4

    1. Kal Tire (Firm)—History. 2. Tire industry—Canada—History.
3. Service industries—Canada. 4. Franchises (Retail trade)—Canada.
I. Title.

HD9161.5.T574K35 2012   338.7'678320971   C2011-908543-7

CREATIVE DIRECTOR John Wellwood
WRITERS Wayne Lilley, Eve Rockett
DESIGNER Cathy Smith
PHOTO EDITORS Eve Rockett, Alison Pryer
PRODUCTION COORDINATOR Kate Moore
COPYEDITOR Lesley Cameron
PROOFREADER Renate Preuss

Printed in Canada

THIS BOOK IS DEDICATED TO THE MEMORY OF TOM FOORD. HIS VISION, DETERMINATION AND BELIEF IN EMPOWERING OTHERS TO SUCCEED IS A LEGACY FOR US ALL.

IF YOU WANT TO MEET THE MAN

When Bob Wallis arrived at the offices of Kal Tire in Vernon, B.C., on a January morning in 2001, he didn't expect to spend much more than 15 minutes or so over a coffee with Archie Stroh and Ken Finch, two of Kal's senior managers and partners. Kal had been looking for an experienced executive to replace Larry Wynn, its long-time chief financial officer (CFO), who was retiring. Bob had applied for the job and Kal invited him to Vernon so he could become a little better acquainted with Kal, and Kal's executives with him.

Bob certainly didn't lack experience. As a partner in an energy company in Calgary in the 1970s, he'd experienced the vagaries of the oil patch. He'd rebounded from that to become CFO of the information technology company MacDonald Dettwiler in Vancouver. From there he moved into the service industry as CFO of the Milestones restaurant chain.

Bob didn't know much about the tire business — or about Kal for that matter, except by reputation — but his first impression wasn't of a flashy outfit. The low, grey head office building, in an industrial district in the north end of Vernon, gave the impression of a pragmatic company that valued function over form. The impression was reinforced inside where the atmosphere was casually comfortable, yet with a distinct air of quiet efficiency.

The same could be said of the Kal partners hosting Bob's visit, despite their different personalities. Archie Stroh, the company's burly senior vice-president and general manager, was as effusive as Ken Finch, Kal's lanky senior vice-president and managing partner, was quietly droll. Bob had taken part in enough business meetings in his career — at the time, he was CFO of the Vancouver-based Spectra Group, an operator of restaurant chains — to anticipate cautious responses to his questions. "But these guys didn't hide anything," he says. "They just came across as sincere and confident."

Bob admits that he wondered at first if any business could care as much about customers and employees as Kal claimed to. He noticed that Ken and Archie — and indeed most Kal employees — became near evangelical when discussing the company's values and principles. "Tires and profits seemed to be the last thing they were concerned with when describing Kal's business model," he says. "They wanted to talk about Kal's culture and the belief that team member satisfaction began with training that added to their skill set and generated self-respect and confidence."

Bob was skeptical. What Kal claimed as the defining elements of its culture didn't initially sound too different from claims he had heard others cite as the secret of their success. However, he soon realized that the difference at Kal was the hard evidence that it had more than paid lip service to its principles and been repaid into the bargain: the company had sales of nearly half a billion dollars, yet little debt, and its profit-sharing plan, which contributed 50 percent of its profits to employees' retirement funds, was the most generous that Bob had ever encountered. And what was more, Kal had a base plan that benefited everyone in the company.

Bob's surprise continued to grow as Ken and Archie met all his queries with the plain-spoken sincerity he was beginning to recognize as Kal's corporate character — even if the delivery varied between Archie's feisty assertiveness and Ken's quiet erudition. What did Kal's business model look like? The managers of its decentralized outlets operated relatively autonomously and were overseen by zone managers. They, in turn, were supervised by senior zone managers.

Not so different, Bob mused, from systems he had seen and even worked under in the past. "Yes, but zone managers and senior managers in those systems probably didn't also manage stores, which gives our guys credibility as well as a model store to demonstrate the right way to do things," said Archie. As Bob reflected on that statement, he realized, "I'd never heard of zone managers and senior zone managers also being store managers," he says. "When I thought about it, I realized it was brilliant."

When Bob wondered how Kal perpetuated and spread its culture as it grew, Ken told him that visits from senior managers, the zone management system and an extensive in-house training program all helped. "When he mentioned the AIMS as being vital as well, I made the usual mistake and thought they were a mission statement," says Bob. "I'd seen lots of those that didn't work."

Ken quickly and eloquently alleviated Bob's skepticism, explaining that the AIMS are a set of core values that Kal employees accept as a code that guides their behaviour and approach to their duties. Far from being a goal or target like a mission statement, the AIMS invite self-assessment to turn employees' focus outward toward the customers.

By the time Archie and Ken were through pointing out the likelihood of Kal perpetuating its alchemy of stability and growth — as a private, family-owned company, it has the luxury of looking farther down the road without concerning itself about such things as a volatile stock price or a hostile takeover — they'd sold Bob on Kal. "All I could think was, where do I sign?" he says.

Archie and Ken were pleased that Bob Wallis, an impressively qualified candidate, was interested in Kal. But there was a final hurdle to be cleared. Kal's policy was that no matter what position an employee would eventually be in, he or she had to experience the gritty operating end of the tire business first. How did Bob feel about changing tires or crawling around under trucks at the side of the road while working out of a Kal store for a while?

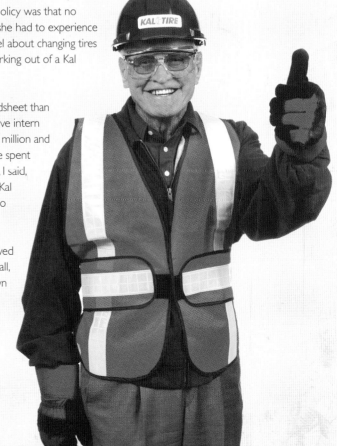

Needless to say, Bob was more comfortable working with a spreadsheet than a drop sheet. But he couldn't argue with the results of Kal's executive intern program. The company, then in its 47th year, had revenues of $400 million and was still growing rapidly. "I told them I could deal with that, the time spent working in the store," he says. "Then when we were shaking hands, I said, 'From what you guys have told me, I can't see there's much about Kal that I'd change. I don't know what the model for all this was, or who inspired it, but it's amazing.'"

Archie and Ken explained that Kal Tire's business model had evolved over the years, "but if you want to meet the man who inspired it all, come on, we'll go and see if he's in." Just like that, they set off down the hall.

"That's when I met Kal Tire's founder, Tom Foord," says Bob. "The guy who had been Kal's first president for 46 years."

In front of the
original Kal Tire store
in the late 1950s,
(L-R) Jim Lochhead,
Charlie Stackand and
Tom Foord.

CHAPTER ONE:
THE EARLY YEARS

(1905–1954)

> **"** No matter how hard you tried to succeed, nothing ever seemed to work. If it wasn't the weather, it was the price of grain beating you down ... Everywhere I looked I saw nothing but failure. **"**

LIFE ON
THE PRAIRIES

Tom Foord's father, Albert, known as Bert, was born in Bristol, England. The son of a prosperous cattle farmer and businessman, Bert went to only the best schools. In 1905, he and his older brother, Sid, abandoned privilege in favour of adventure and emigrated to Canada. Attracted by government offers of free land to homesteaders, the brothers ended up in the village of Instow, Saskatchewan, in 1905, the same year that Saskatchewan became a Canadian province.

Life on the Canadian prairies was not for the faint of heart. An English public school education was of scant use when it came to building a one-room sod home, enduring the perishing cold of a Saskatchewan winter or establishing a farm. When the brothers' father arrived for a visit in 1912, he surveyed the prairie landscape from the train, pronounced his sons crazy for staying in such a desolate land and then headed back home without ever disembarking. By then, though, the brothers were confirmed Canadian farmers. Bert sealed his commitment to life in Canada in 1919 when he married Emma, a woman 15 years his junior who lived on a neighbouring farm. In 1922, their son Tom was born.

The Foords got by — in some cases better than their neighbours — and Tom grew up amidst relative prosperity. His father's ambition during the Great Depression saw him taking jobs as the postmaster, the local agent who handled payment to local farmers for their grain and a supplier of fuel to his neighbours. Bert's gas pump was unmanned; customers recorded what they bought and paid later. "The system, based on trust, worked just fine," says Tom.

In a sense, Tom's childhood into his teens was an iconic example of life on the Canadian prairies before World War II. Entertainment was homemade, with the highlight being the arrival of Eaton's catalogue every spring and fall. By 1936, radio shows such as *Gangbusters* were fuelling Tom's 14-year-old imagination and attracting neighbours to the Foords' place, as they were one of the few families to own a radio.

However, nothing could compare to Tom's love for hockey. After school and farm chores, he grabbed his skates and stick to become vicariously one of the hockey heroes whom Foster Hewitt described during Saturday evening broadcasts of Maple Leaf games from Toronto. "I was four when I started skating," says Tom. "Every winter I spent hours every day skating with a hockey stick in my hand." The radio, he adds, also played a role in his unaccountable passion for dancing. "I don't know where I got it, but I had this need to dance when I heard music," he says.

Clockwise from top left: Tom's grandmother Julia Beeker Foord. Tom at the age of two with his mother Emma, father Bert, and baby brother Vernon, in 1924. The Foord family in Instow (L-R) Bert, Emma, Emma's brother Walter, her mother Mary, Uncle Stanley holding young Tom, and a friend, circa 1924. Grandfather James Foord in England, circa 1880s.

13

Although only a teen at the nadir of the Depression in 1937, Tom nonetheless recalls its demoralizing effect on the community around him. "Everybody was broke, and some people were poorer than others," says Tom. "No matter how hard you tried to succeed, nothing ever seemed to work. If it wasn't the weather, it was the price of grain beating you down … Everywhere I looked I saw nothing but failure."

The drought, heat and plagues of grasshoppers that struck the prairies were symptomatic of the dire straits into which the entire country had plunged. The charity that his mother extended to jobless men who "rode the rods" of freight trains in and out of town while seeking jobs stuck with Tom all his life. "I'd be sitting on the front steps and all these men would come around," he says. "I never forgot how grateful they were when they sat down with me, gobbled up their sandwiches, gave their thanks and then went on their way again."

Tom, too, had an impatient energy that kept him on the go — and that poorly suited him to school, his obvious intelligence notwithstanding. "Nothing happened fast enough," he remembers. "You had to work a whole year to pass a grade, and I was always trying to be ahead of myself and get to where I thought I should be."

By the time he reached his mid-teens, restless and bored after only eight years' schooling, Tom put Instow's one-room school behind him. His self-described "desperation to succeed" prompted him to give education another try via correspondence courses, but he eventually abandoned it for good. "All school meant to me was self-discipline," he says. "And I lacked that terribly."

All school meant to me was self-discipline, and I lacked that terribly.

ROMANCE IN THE TELETYPE OFFICE

Canada's entry to World War II presented Tom with both an adventure and an opportunity to fulfill his longtime wish — to become a pilot. In 1940, at age 18, he joined the Royal Canadian Air Force and was assigned to flight school. However, flying in the RCAF was not to be. A flight instructor disputed Tom's confidence in his own skills, and ended Tom's flight training. "He constantly gave me hell in the air," he says. "In his eyes I couldn't do anything right. It wasn't a lot of fun."

The air force didn't exactly satisfy his hope for adventure, either. Though Tom's first posting was his first time outside Canada, he notes with a laugh that it was only to the air force teletype office in St. John's, Newfoundland — still nine years away from joining Confederation.

While the setting didn't especially excite the teen, Norah Davidson, a pretty stenographer from Vernon, B.C., who worked at the site, did. Their first date was a lobster dinner at the Newfoundland Hotel that cost $1.00 a plate, and Tom remembers it as intimidating. "I'm a flatlander and we weren't used to lobsters," he says. "I couldn't figure out how to get at it, or how to eat it."

Tom's anxiety didn't seem to put Norah off, though, as the couple were eventually engaged. Following their engagement, Tom made his first trip to Vernon, B.C., to meet Norah's parents. He returned to St. John's after a week, delighted by Norah's father, a sheep rancher, and her mother, a concert pianist. "They had imagination and a culture they had brought with them from Scotland, and I wanted to be part of their life," he says. And he'd been just as smitten by the mountains and hills that enclosed the town in the Okanagan Valley. "It had been fruit time and apple trees were everywhere," he says. "My memory of Saskatchewan was the drought, when you couldn't grow a carrot. Vernon was heaven in comparison. I was anxious to get back there, even if I didn't have a job."

Above, from left:
Norah in her WWII uniform, completely happy and at home in the air force. One of the flocks on the Davidson ranch in summertime.
Opposite, from top:
Norah's parents, Jane and Robert, with family dog Coolin in their backyard, circa 1930s. Norah and Tom's romance began slowly; they became fast friends before falling in love.

MAKING A HOME IN VERNON

Tom and Norah married on July 16, 1944, in Calgary, midway between Vernon and Instow so that both sets of parents could attend the ceremony. When the war ended in 1945, the couple moved to Vernon to live with Norah's parents. Unsure of what he was going to do, Tom worked briefly in his father-in-law's sheep ranching business, then took a job with Home Oil, delivering heating fuel.

When Norah's mother died in 1949, the couple used a government War Veterans' Allowance as collateral for a $6,000 mortgage and built a home in Vernon. Tom's characteristic plunging into the project without adequate planning or monitoring costs proved a mistake. In short order, cost overruns hit $2,300. "I had no idea what it cost to build anything," Tom admits, "and I was only making $120 a month driving the truck."

As grim as the prospect of foreclosure was, the incident became a part of the belated education of Tom Foord. To deal with his debt, Tom visited his creditors and persuaded each of them to accept $25 a month. True to his word, he never missed a payment. He also learned how to negotiate with banks. "And a good thing, too," he cracks today. "One way or another I stayed on their hook for 25 years in business."

In the meantime, Tom took a job selling Kirby vacuum cleaners door-to-door to earn more money. His facility for sales, however, was hampered by his conscience — at least in the company's view. On one occasion Tom sold a machine to a woman who had no carpets and only one electrical outlet in the house. Two months later she approached the company for a refund.

Despite the company's protests, Tom insisted she be given her money back. "My thinking was, Kirby might lose the immediate sale, but in the long term, it would have a lifelong supporter and that would probably sell a lot more vacuums," Tom says. The ethics of dealing fairly with customers and the logic of long-term thinking would eventually become guiding principles in Tom's stunningly successful business career. However, putting them into practice at Kirby soon saw him back driving a fuel delivery truck.

Fortunately, when Home Oil promoted him from truck driver to warehouse supervisor Tom was able to make up the income from the vacuum cleaner sales. But while his new job responsibilities paid more, and included responsibility for inventory and branch operations, both useful skills, when Home Oil offered him a job in commercial sales in Vancouver, he turned it down. "I'd pretty much decided that if I was ever going to find out if I could make it on my own, I'd better get on with it," he says.

THE BUDDING ENTREPRENEUR

The object of Tom's start-up plans was a Vernon Home Oil service station on the verge of bankruptcy. Convinced he could save it, Tom raised $450 by cashing in his pension and borrowed $900 from the bank and $1,500 from Norah's father. The business was so stretched financially that when it opened in May 1951 Tom had to borrow $20 from the former owner as a float for the till so he could make change. Still, the venture showed promise; on his first day in business, Tom actually made enough money to pay back the $20.

The 29-year-old's euphoria gradually wore off, however, as he realized why his predecessor had almost gone bankrupt. There was quite simply no business activity in the location. Tom was willing to spend 7 days a week, 14 hours a day on the job, but no customers meant no money. "Only someone as naive as me would ever have attempted to start a business with no money or resources to weather any kind of adversity," Tom says in retrospect. "Everybody in Vernon was in the gasoline business in those days. If a guy had a grocery store, he put a pump outside. There were as many gas outlets in town as there were churches."

It was bad enough, he adds, that competition drove prices down and sliced margins razor thin, but you had to work just as hard as if you were making a nice profit. "Most people bought two dollars' worth of gas," Tom says. "But to get that sale you had to check the radiator and the fan belt, take a look at the battery, check the tires and wash the windows."

Tom credits Norah with keeping him going. "I'd go home and tell her I'd made the biggest mistake of my life," he says, "but the more anxious I got, the more calming she was. She never stopped believing."

His suppliers, however, weren't so sanguine. Two years after Tom bought the business, MacKenzie, White and Dunsmuir, his auto-parts supplier, was threatening to shut him down if he didn't pay the arrears on his account. Despite his lack of credit room with the bank, Tom still believed in his power of persuasion. In a letter to the company, he acknowledged his position and committed to repaying his debts. Perhaps sensing his sincerity, his creditor extended him a lifeline and agreed to continue to give him credit.

More valuable than the money, Tom says, was the lesson he learned. "I don't know why they showed faith in me, but when they did, it made me more determined than ever to repay them," he says. "It was something I never forgot. Respect for and fair treatment of customers and suppliers was a principle I followed throughout my entire career."

From top: Tom's service station, which he renamed Home Terminal and then transformed into the first Kal Tire store two years later — this photo was taken in 1928, 23 years before Tom bought it. The original Kal Tire store in the late 1950s.

From top: When biscuit salesman Jim Lochhead (left) confided to Tom that he had $8,000 to invest, it was the beginning of a great business partnership and the birth of Kal Tire. A receipt for work done at Tom's first garage in Vernon. An early Uniroyal brochure used by Kal Tire.

NAME E.L. LEEK VERNON
DATE MAY 25
PHONE
ADDRESS
LICENSE
MILEAGE
CAR MAKE Mercury
SAE No.

Gals. Home Gas
Qts. Home Motor Oil
Protexal Chassis Lubrication — 4 60
1 25
One CIIA-2853 Cable. 85
Charge Battery 2 25
Test Generator
Tire Repairs 8 95
Labour.

AS ADDED SERVICE WE HAVE CHECKED:
MOTOR OIL | TIRES | BATTERY | RADIATOR
TRANSMISS. | WIND. WIPER | BAT. CABLES | RAD. HOSE
DIFFER'IAL | AIR CLEANER | LIGHTS | FAN BEL

COMMENTS

ENDLY HOME GAS DEALER

Introducing...the new
UNIROYAL MASTER
(THE TIRE FOR WORRIERS)

UNIROYAL

THE BIRTH OF
KAL TIRE

Two years after going into business for himself, Tom was still keeping the doors open, but only barely and with little enthusiasm. "It's not much fun owning a business when nothing you do seems to make it work," he says. "I was looking out the window at the cars and trucks going by one afternoon, thinking, 'All I'm doing is spinning my wheels; I'm not getting anywhere,' when it suddenly hit me. Maybe it was the idea of spinning wheels, but all I could think was, 'Everything runs on rubber!' After that, I knew that tires were the answer."

From the outset Tom was pretty sure he didn't want to repeat his service station mistake and get into a business selling the same thing as everyone else. Unlike gasoline, which was basically the same for everyone, tires came in different sizes for different vehicles. And in any case, as Tom thought through his epiphany he began to see tire service, rather than the tires themselves, as the way he could differentiate himself from competitors.

Tom's gregarious nature frequently turned his service station customers into friends. He enjoyed batting ideas around with biscuit company salesman Jim Lochhead who often dropped by with product samples and stayed for coffee. From their conversations, Tom knew that Jim was as bored selling cookies as Tom was frustrated by the service station business. Jim often suggested going into business with Tom if they could come up with something that could support them both.

When Tom repeated his tire revelation and indicated his intention to go into the business as soon as he got some capital together, Jim saw it as the chance to create a partnership. And not only did he agree with Tom about the potential of a tire business based on service, he also had $8,000 to invest and kick-start the venture. Tom recognized an opportunity to develop a project he'd been considering. "It was an amazing turnaround for me," Tom says. "One day I was ready to let the business go and a week later I was standing there, seeing a vision become reality in our new partnership. I thought to myself, 'How lucky can I be?'"

MacKenzie, White and Dunsmuir, which distributed Dominion Royal tires in B.C., advised Tom to start out slowly, to only sell tires and to not bother with mechanical services. To Tom, though, that sounded like tiptoeing into the business, which was not his way. "This was dream stuff," says Tom, "and I was going into the business whole hog or not at all."

Tom's vision, as he laid it out to Jim, his new partner, was an operation that went where the customers were, even if it meant heading into the bush to reach forestry companies or out on the highways to change blown tires on trucks. He wanted to include vulcanizing services to repair tires and a retreading operation that recapped customers' tire casings, adding to their service life. "Jim thought it all sounded good so we decided to do it," he says.

Tom's bank manager, however, was not impressed with Tom's idea of opening a tire store in partnership with a biscuit salesman. But Tom insisted that the honesty and integrity he'd shown in honouring his obligations to repay bank loans, plus his and Jim's willingness to work hard, were all virtues that would underpin their business, ensuring its success. And of course, he says now with a twinkle in his eye, "There was also Jim's $8,000 investment. Bankers won't give you loans if you need it, only when they know you already have some money."

The new partners turned out to have complementary talents. Tom was an aggressive extrovert who knew the operating end of the business and would be the front man. Jim had qualities beyond those Tom described to the bank manager. "Jim had a sense of humour, he was great with numbers and he was frugal," says Tom of the man who would be his partner for 19 years.

> *All I'm doing is spinning my wheels; I'm not getting anywhere, when it suddenly hit me. Maybe it was the idea of spinning wheels, but all I could think was, 'Everything runs on rubber!' After that, I knew that tires were the answer.*

"He wouldn't waste anything, and this was a good characteristic when we didn't have anything to waste." Most important, Tom adds, Jim had already proven himself an excellent biscuit salesman, and he turned out to be just as good at selling tires and associated services — "which is a very good thing when you're starting off with zero sales."

Reconfiguring the service station into a tire centre that included retread equipment was the first order of the day. Home Oil owned the real estate. To add an extension for retreading, the partners had to buy the three lots next door. But because Home Oil owned the original property, they couldn't get a mortgage. Tom approached Home Oil seeking an agreement that would allow him and Jim to sell their product through the store for 15 years.

With that deal in hand, the bank relented and Tom and Jim got a mortgage to purchase the whole piece of property, plus the three lots for $300 each. Tom borrowed $10,000 to buy the retreading equipment, establishing a relationship with Dominion Rubber — which would become Uniroyal — that lasted into the early 1970s.

On June 12, 1953, Tom and Jim opened their first store. They called the business Kal Tire, honouring Kalamalka Lake (known as the lake of many colours) near Vernon, Tom Foord's adopted hometown. The partners agreed that Tom would be president and Jim vice-president. Tom's wife, Norah, was the secretary and Jim's wife, Mary, was the treasurer. Kal was a family operation in the truest sense of the term. Mary, as it turned out, had played a critical role in the company's founding. The $8,000 in seed money that

Jim had put up was her inheritance. Kal paid the wives a minimal wage for their corporate duties, "and they still expect us to wash their work overalls," Mary cheerily complained during one of the twice-a-month phone calls she and Norah made to commiserate with each other at being spouses of entrepreneurs.

This time there was no slow beginning, and no need to borrow money for change as Tom had done two years earlier. From the start, he knew he'd found his calling at Kal. "I smelled success from the first day," he maintains. He and Jim had known from the beginning that they'd need something to differentiate Kal from their many competitors in the tire business.

"As soon as we started thinking 'service' we knew we'd hit on the thing we could do better than anyone else," says Tom.

CHAPTER TWO: BIG TREADS, GOOD TRACTION

(1953–1969)

> " Rogers Pass is where we cut our teeth. I went to the sites myself, changed tires and got in on the ground floor. "

KAL FINDS
ITS NICHE

Most of Kal Tire's competitors were relatively diversified, typically dealing also with brakes, mufflers and mechanical repairs. Many were filling stations as well. But when it came to tires, they mainly concentrated on the car and light-truck market, and paid less attention to tires that truckers or logging companies used on off-road equipment. "The commercial side was the weakest aspect of their business," says Tom, "and their service and marketing were practically non-existent."

There was a good reason for that, of course. Retail customers were the proverbial low-hanging fruit — they drove up to a tire store when they needed tires. Commercial customers, however, tended to be inconveniently located and expensive to reach with a marketing message. It was also difficult to service commercial customers with delivery, repair and retreading. "Many were forestry operations, logging and sawmills typically well off the highway with little that could be described as a main road of any kind," Tom says. "They made heavy demands on the tires on their off-the-road (OTR) equipment, however. So while the customers were hard to reach, we saw an opportunity to offer them service."

The partners split their duties. Jim spent most of his time on the road looking for new business among truckers. Tom tended to their existing business, handling service calls to forest industry camps. His message was consistent: no matter how remote the camps' location, Kal Tire was interested in their business. Within a year of its founding, Kal backed up its claim by opening its first branch: a one-man operation in Nakusp, east of Vernon.

The expansion had nothing to do with growth for growth's sake, Tom emphasizes. The Nakusp location was decidedly modest, set up in a building rented for $60 a month, but it was near two of Kal's good customers, Celgar Pulp Company and Eagle Sawmills (later bought by Columbia Cellulose). Tom had already decided that Kal needed to be where its customers were, a maxim that would guide its growth for more than half a century.

The more Tom and Jim looked, the more market opportunities they saw. The 150 sawmills around Revelstoke, Vernon and Nakusp all had to send their people into town whenever they needed a retread, blew a tire or required a new tire. Kal saw this as an opportunity and offered delivery as well as repair service in the field.

The launching of Kal dramatically changed the Foord family's life. As customer satisfaction increased, so did Tom's workload. An order for four tires meant loading the tires onto the truck and driving for miles down rugged logging roads. It also meant leaving Norah and the kids — they now had four children, Jean, Colin, Nancy and Janet; a second son, Robert, arrived four years later. Sometimes inclement weather forced him to stay away overnight, but he would put those evenings to good use, forging relationships that he intuitively knew were the lifeblood of growing a service business. When not on customer sites, he toured nearby towns looking for stores that he and Jim could buy and reopen under the Kal Tire banner, creating more branches that would be closer to their customers.

Tom was often away for days at a time. Norah took care of the children and provided Tom and Kal with unwavering support. "To be successful you have to give the business your undivided attention and think about it day and night," Tom says. "This isn't possible unless your family is taken care of, and that's what Norah did. Norah always backed me up and she never pried or criticized. Unlike some businessmen I know, I never came home to an argument about being short of money or that the business wasn't going to make it. With Norah, I always felt I had a shoulder to lean on."

BREAKTHROUGH IN ROGERS PASS

As busy as the partners had been, Kal was still very much a work in progress five years after its start-up. But Tom and Jim had accomplished enough to assure themselves that they were on the right track. Their faith was rewarded in 1958 when Tom drove up to Revelstoke, east of Vernon on the Canadian Pacific Railway rail line, to scout out a new store location.

While there, he heard that the superintendent of General Construction was staying at the local railroad hotel. The company had contracts to work on the Trans-Canada Highway being built through Rogers Pass between Revelstoke in the west and Golden to the east. Tom headed straight for the superintendent's room, seeking to secure the company's tire business. Tom's gift for spontaneous rapport paid off when the man promised to recommend Kal to his company's general manager in Vancouver.

Excited by the new business prospect, Tom headed home. As he drove along a road under construction, the air thick with dust, he didn't see the car that was heading straight for him. He woke up later in the hospital with a badly gashed head. An RCMP officer offered to phone Norah, but the phone lines were down. The officer subsequently got sidetracked and forgot about making the call. Two days later Norah still didn't know what had happened to her husband.

A worried Jim finally tracked Tom down and phoned Norah. When Norah asked how he was, Jim told her, "He's okay, but he has a little hole in his head." The way Jim recounts the tale, a relieved Norah paused only a fraction of a second before responding, "That's fine then. He had a hole in his head when he left."

The story, like so many Tom was involved in, ended happily. He recovered quickly, kept his appointment in Vancouver with General Construction and came away with a contract for Kal to supply and service all the company's OTR tires in Rogers Pass for the next three years.

A truck hoisting tires at a site in the late 1950s.

It was easily the biggest piece of business Kal Tire had secured in its five-year existence. And it gave Kal some welcome credibility. A major contracting company had endorsed the business, in effect declaring Kal a knowledgeable and serious contender in the OTR tire market in B.C., but it would all be for naught if Kal didn't perform. The contract meant an increased workload, especially for Kal's principals. "Rogers Pass is where we cut our teeth," says Tom. "I went to the sites myself, changed tires and got in on the ground floor. By the time mining and logging industries took off a couple of years later, we already had the experience to take advantage of the opportunities."

Working in Rogers Pass, notorious for avalanches, was no picnic. Marginal roads meant all equipment had to be transported by train. To get to the camp in his four-wheel-drive truck, Tom forded creeks and crashed through snowdrifts. He stayed in a bunkhouse whose inhabitants were determinedly suspicious of both outsiders and each other, all the while living in close quarters. "Mealtimes were a stampede to the dining room to get there first, and you never sat beside the same man twice," says Tom. "There was no conversation; it was eat and get out. I remember sitting beside one fellow who devoured 22 lamb chops in total silence in eight minutes."

LEARNING ON THE JOB

The learning curve on the project was as steep as the road up to the pass, and it left about as much room for error. Equipment downtime was costly for the customer, so getting it back into action as soon as possible was paramount. A more experienced man might have found Tom's challenges fairly routine, but because he had no background in working on a job on the scale of the Rogers Pass project, Tom had to innovate to overcome problems. In the absence of proper equipment to handle the immense wheels and tires, he rigged cables and come-alongs to mount on scrapers, loaders and dump trucks.

Occasionally, though, he faced tasks that defied even his ingenuity. On one occasion, while shimming a wheel and tire with a block of wood to line it up to be mounted on a loader, Tom discovered it was still out of line by a few inches. When he tried using the loader's own gin-pole hoist to assist him, the wood he'd used jumped out of place and went through the vehicle's windshield, under his arm and into the seat.

"I was still alive, but now I had two problems: the tire and the windshield," he says. "The union wouldn't allow drivers to work without a windshield, and there must have been a hundred screws holding the plastic shield on. I worked on it all night, all by myself, taking it off. Then I got my hands on a new windshield, installed it, put the tire on. I finished up just before the men came in to work at 7:00 a.m. I was a total rube, a dumbbell. But I was learning, and I got the job done."

Above, from left:
The Kal Tire team on site in Rogers Pass, late 1950s. Tom and a Kal Tire employee in front of one of the early Kal Tire service trucks, at Rogers Pass in 1958.

Tom's experience, along with a serious accident involving Kal's mechanic, Andy Stinn, underscored the danger on the job. While doing a routine tire inflation, the chuck of the hose came off the valve stem. Andy put it back on, but with the wrong-sized o-ring on the lock ring. "The tire blew up, seriously damaging Andy's head," Tom says. "It was an awful sight and you can imagine the commotion around the camp. We thought he was a dead man." Andy had to be taken to hospital in Golden by train, and from there by ambulance to Calgary. Tom chartered a plane to fly Andy's wife to Calgary where Andy was unconscious for six days.

Andy's accident had at least one positive outcome: it helped move safety to the top of Kal's priority list. Tom tightened operating regulations and changed a number of procedures to make them safer. To prevent injury from blowouts, for example, Kal adopted a system of using chains to secure tires while they were being inflated.

But safety wasn't always the easiest sell in the macho world of tires, despite plenty of evidence that the business was dangerous for anyone who ignored proper techniques. The hapless Andy Stinn proved the case. The poster boy for dogged loyalty when he recovered from his head injury and promptly returned to work, Andy was cited for carelessness soon after his return. He had failed to use safety chains on a tire he was inflating, and it blew. "It came off the rim, banged against the wall, bounced back and hit him right in the chest," says Tom. "When he came to, he had three broken ribs. I guess he hadn't learned his lesson."

When Prime Minister John Diefenbaker officially opened the Rogers Pass highway in 1962, Kal could be justly proud of its contribution to the construction of one of Canada's most important east-west trade routes. More important for Kal, though, was the way it had become involved and the grit with which it had performed. The company validated "seize all opportunities" as a worthy addition to the growing list of maxims and best practices that were becoming standard operating procedure at Kal.

HEAD OFFICE IN A DUPLEX

In some ways, Kal seemed almost caught off guard by its own success. Its crowded head office in the early 1960s reflected its focus on growing operations that made money, with less regard for the administrative side that looked after it. The company's headquarters consisted of six people squeezed into a unit in a duplex across the street from the Kal Tire retread plant in Vernon.

According to Maggie Morrice, hired as a bookkeeper to track each day's business, the office wasn't much quieter than a retread plant at times. She remembers the clatter of her huge Burroughs calculator, sounding like a train going through the building. Tom's office was in the unit's bedroom; to get to the washroom, every employee had to pass his desk. Jack Kristensen, the office manager, worked on a table in the kitchen.

There was no shortage of things to do. Sales and service had both picked up during Kal's involvement in the Rogers Pass project, and neither slowed much afterwards. Maintaining cash flow required paying close attention to receivables. It wasn't uncommon for Jack Kristensen to enlist Tom's assistance to confront customers who had outstanding accounts, or to pay a surprise visit to a store to do a thorough inventory. Kal's practice was to give every employee a set of tires every year — but that didn't stop the odd set of tires from rolling mysteriously out the door, costing the company thousands of dollars.

AIR KAL

Despite having had his flying ambitions thwarted in his air force days, Tom continued to nurture a yearning to get his pilot's licence. In 1960, he signed up for lessons with Frank Talbot, a Vernon-based bush pilot. Tom justified this undertaking on the grounds that it would be good for business. Instead of spending days driving to small towns throughout northern and central B.C., he reasoned, he'd be able to save time by flying.

Tom quickly disproved his RCAF instructor's previous assessment that he lacked an aptitude for flying. Encouraged by Frank, he took to flying with an enthusiasm that prompted the instructor to dub him Fearless Foord. Within weeks of getting his licence, Tom took the next step: through Kal, he bought a four-seat Cessna 172.

Unable to resist Tom's evangelical enthusiasm for flight, Jim Lochhead also learned to fly. Jim never quite came to share Tom's infatuation with flight, Tom acknowledges, which was consistent with the partners' different temperaments: to Tom, an inveterate risk-taker, encountering fog when flying was a challenge; to the more cautious Jim, a year and a half older than Tom, fog was a major concern, terrifying even. "If Jim couldn't see Kelowna from Vernon," Tom laughs, "he wouldn't take off."

The company plane soon proved to be the business tool Tom had hoped it would become. He and Jim could cover much more territory in a single day, calling on potential customers and servicing existing ones, and scouting new store locations. Four-day trips were cut to one. "Airplanes helped build Kal Tire," says Archie Stroh, who joined Kal in 1970 and stayed for more than 30 years. "They gave us a huge step up on our competitors. We could get to isolated places in hours when it used to take days by car. And being able to get home from a business trip on schedule instead of spending another day or night away probably saved a lot of marriages at Kal."

Identifying the benefit to Kal of a single plane made it easier to first add more planes and then to exchange them later for faster ones with a longer range as Kal grew its business and spread geographically. The Cessna 172 was followed by a single-engine Cessna 210 with retractable landing gear for faster flying speeds. ("Tom and I literally lived in that 210 for five years," says Archie.) The Cessna 210 was traded for a twin-engined Cessna 320, then a pair of six-seat, twin-engined Cessna 340s.

Cessna Conquest twin-engined turboprop planes were then bought in partnership with a forestry company. The planes' 1,200-mile range and 300-mile-per-hour speed enabled Kal to cover its growing network across the West. Kal's purchase of two Cessna Citation jets, capable of crossing the country at 500 miles an hour were the cornerstones of Kal aviation in 2008, their range and speed reflecting the far-flung nature of Kal's business.

Kal still has the Cessna 210. "Tom didn't fly in his later years," says Archie. "He just didn't like to get rid of anything. But he had more than 10,000 flying hours, which was a big accomplishment for a private pilot."

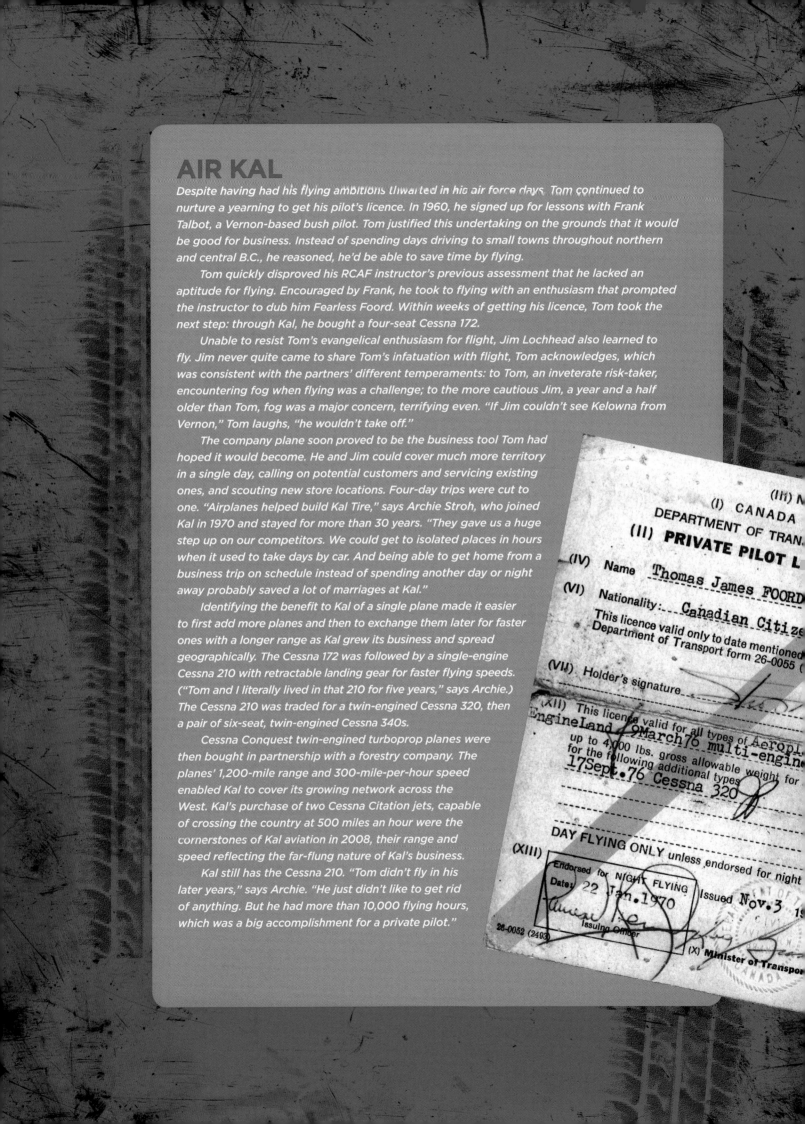

Jack Kristensen points out that Tom and Jim's initial dream had been to become the biggest tire company in the Okanagan Valley. After only 10 years, they'd mostly achieved that. Along with its four primary outlets in Nakusp, Vernon, Penticton and Kamloops, Kal had a retread plant associated with the Kamloops store, both of which were run by the faithful Colin Campbell. In 1963, Kal opened a branch store in Williams Lake, followed by outlets in Prince George, Vanderhoof and Fort St. James. For every opening, Tom, Jim, Jack Kristensen and Bill Fleming, who managed the Vernon store, flew in for a ceremony and coffee and cookies.

Flying was, in some respects, an expression of Tom's personality. He had the technical capability to be a fine pilot, but occasionally overlooked details. Once, on his way to a meeting, he absent-mindedly tossed his suit over the tail of the plane and forgot about it when he climbed aboard — until he got a call from the tower telling him it was on the runway. Despite occasionally losing his way, or landing with a fuel gauge pointing near empty, Tom's confidence never wavered, even if his passengers tended to clutch their armrests and close their eyes as he cheerfully aimed for a hole in the clouds to make a landing.

Jack Kristensen, who made frequent trips with Tom, recalls his boss's unnerving habit of handing the controls over to his passengers. "He told me to take the wheel, set the course on compass, keep the plane at the same height and fly," Jack says. "Then he lay back and dozed off. It was a big thrill for me." Tom's habit was more terror-inducing than thrilling for some, though. Archie Stroh, who joined Kal in 1970, also recalls becoming one of Tom's impromptu co-pilots before he became a pilot himself.

THE BEST BUSINESSMAN KAL TIRE NEVER HIRED

Far from regretting his lack of formal education, Tom made up for it by exercising his curiosity. Once he discovered that most experienced businesspeople shared his inquisitiveness, he took advantage. "I was always looking to educate myself," he says, "and top-notch people became my mentors. I was friendly and curious about everything they had to offer. Maybe that's the reason George Miller took a liking to me." Whatever the reason, the relationship between the two men would become one of the most important in Tom's life and in the evolution of Kal Tire.

Tom and George met for the first time in 1960 when Tom was negotiating the acquisition of the Williams Lake store, north of Kamloops in B.C.'s Interior. An accountant whom Tom called for advice recommended that Tom contact George Miller, an experienced businessman and senior partner in a Vancouver accounting firm that would become KPMG. After speaking with him, George agreed to accompany Tom to Williams Lake.

Tom Foord considers one of his strengths to be "knowing what I don't know. So I always looked for help from people who knew more than I did." George Miller certainly knew more than Tom about finance at that time. After closing the Williams Lake deal, George remained at Tom's side for almost 40 years — through meetings with suppliers and negotiations with banks, and in every acquisition from small-town independents to giant tire chains — as the two men formed one of the most enduring bonds in Canadian business. Remarkably, George never became a Kal employee, but he would play a crucial role in the company's evolution.

Although their personalities and actions often appeared different, their characters complemented one another. George was as tough in negotiations as Tom could be casual. He preferred staring down opponents to Tom's more conciliatory ways. "I trusted George and hung onto him like you wouldn't believe," says Tom. "He could be rough, but put him in any president's office and he was instantly respected."

Opposite: Kinsmen president Tom Foord with Vernon mayor Frank Telfer, presenting a new ambulance to the city in March 1960.

Part of Tom's admiration for George was a response to the self-discipline his friend had demonstrated in overcoming his twin demons, alcohol and tobacco. George's ultimate victory over both later encouraged Tom to extend a helping hand to others similarly afflicted and in whom he saw promise. "George," says Tom, "had an unbelievably strong will."

Archie Stroh says George's will manifested itself not just in business on Kal's behalf, but in his personal tussles with the equally strong-willed Tom. Archie still marvels at how the two thrashed out differences of opinion with apparently no rules of engagement. "They'd go at it, head to head, bang, bang, bang, for a couple of hours," says Archie. "Then suddenly they'd be laughing and off to lunch together."

The arguments and outcomes, Archie adds, created an environment at Kal that shaped his own approach to business. "It taught me a lot about how to fight it out when you really believe in something, and how to have a constructive disagreement when the goals of both parties are the same — to make things better."

Whatever the reason, the relationship between the two men [George and Tom] would become one of the most important in Tom's life and in the evolution of Kal Tire.

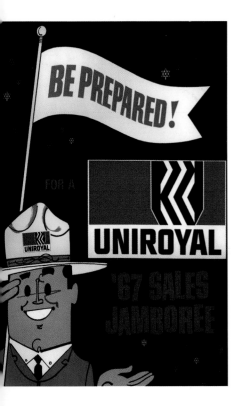

THE DEALER-SUPPLIER GAME

From the day Kal opened, it had been a Uniroyal dealer. During the early years, Tom and Jim maintained a close relationship with their supplier. It was relatively easy to do while they were small and mainly operating in the B.C. Interior, and the arrangement benefited both parties. Kal could count on a consistent supply of products from Uniroyal and receive wholesale discounts based on volume. In turn, Kal represented Uniroyal in markets the rubber company couldn't easily reach and build sales for its products. Part of the deal was that Uniroyal had agreed not to compete with Kal in specific markets, but it did sell directly to end-users in high-volume markets.

As logical as it all seemed, the dealer–supplier arrangements in the tire business were typically fraught with tensions. Concerns on both sides seemed — and still seem — endless. Dealers worried that suppliers would abandon them to deal directly with customers, while suppliers fretted that dealers would find another tire source and leave them with a gap in the distribution chain for their products. If a supplier's salespeople strayed into a dealer's market — to service a major national account, say — the dealer saw it as a violation of the exclusivity agreement. Suppliers, meanwhile, feared that dealers who built enough volume would have too much influence over a market and dictate things like the price of tires, generally the purview of the rubber companies.

Inevitably, as Kal grew its commercial-tire business, it became embroiled in a conflict with a supplier. In part, it was fuelled by Tom's fierce determination to remain independent of any rubber company, bound only to his customers. "I could think of nothing more important than being independent of our suppliers," he says. "But that didn't mean we didn't need them; we needed them in the worst way."

Lacking the financial strength to operate without supplier discounts, Kal concentrated on making itself vital to Uniroyal by building its customer base. But Tom knew Kal was walking the fine line between pleasing its supplier with its sales numbers and upsetting the supplier for the same reason. "Some suppliers didn't like it when a company like Kal Tire had too much market influence," he says. "They were convinced that the tail was starting to wag the dog."

AN OFFER
TO SELL

The forest industry provided the bulk of Kal Tire's business, and Prince George, an eight-hour drive north of Vernon, was the centre of logging country in northern B.C. And while it made sense for Kal to open an outlet there, Tom was well aware that doing so would put it in direct competition with Uniroyal, which had a Prince George store.

In 1968, Tom and Jim decided to open a Kal location in Prince George anyway. While he and Jim were in town negotiating with a dealer to buy his operation, a Uniroyal executive who happened to be staying in the same hotel discovered what he was up to. "To a certain degree, negotiating under Uniroyal's noses in Prince George had been mischievous on my part," Tom confesses. "I wanted to see what they would do.

"But in the end the joke was on me. Two days later the Uniroyal guy was on my doorstep in Vernon, asking if I'd be interested in selling out. They were determined to stop the tail wagging the dog, which shows you how nervous they were that they had helped to create a monster."

The offer came at a critical time for Kal's partners. For the first decade of Kal's existence, Tom and Jim had poured much of their lives into the business. In the last five years, however, things had changed slightly. Since 1963, high-risk mining stocks had increasingly enchanted Tom, but he'd not only failed to get rich quick, he'd also suffered a near wipeout in a market setback. Under the circumstances, getting out of the tire business at 46 and taking a handsome profit — something that had so far eluded him in the stock market — didn't seem like a bad option. When he met the Uniroyal executive in Vernon, he agreed to sell provided that the process began immediately.

Tom waited until the next day to tell Jim what he'd done. He knew his partner well enough to anticipate Jim's response to the news. "Jim was delighted with the idea of selling," says Tom. "He'd worked very hard for nearly 16 years building the business, and he'd received few financial rewards. He looked forward to getting his life back."

Opposite, from left: Uniroyal ad from 1966, Kal Tire's supplier from the beginning until they parted company in the mid-1970s. Much of the business in the early years was with smaller logging firms and the trucking companies that served them. **Above:** A Uniroyal sign hangs outside a Kal Tire outlet.

When George Miller and Tom met with Uniroyal in Montreal in June to iron out the deal's details, they were sure their days in the tire business were nearing an end. Before they left, Uniroyal's president had assured them that the handover day would be July 1 — less than a month away.

Their elation drained away shortly after their return to Vernon. First, Uniroyal Canada claimed its head office in New York was pressuring it to cut the price they had offered for Kal. George and Tom flew east to turn down the lower price in person. Negotiations dragged on for another six months. Then Kal got more ominous news: Uniroyal had appointed a new president.

At dinner in Toronto with the new president, Uniroyal's general manager for Canada (who happened to be the future chairman of Uniroyal International in the U.S.) gave Tom the news he'd feared: Uniroyal had decided to invest in its chemical division and passenger tires rather than the latest radial-ply technology for its commercial tire and OTR business segments. The upshot was that Uniroyal would not be taking on new tire acquisitions after all.

"He asked me what I thought," says Tom. "I'm not a good loser, and I told them 'I think I'm sitting with hypocrites,' and I left for the bar. I had been doing business with Uniroyal for 16 years, and many of the people there were close friends, so the deal falling through bothered me a lot. But in the end, it was a crossroads, the turning point for Kal Tire."

TOM TAKES FULL CONTROL

Back in Vernon, Jim Lochhead was devastated by the news. He was a year and a half older than Tom and was ready to retire. But he'd just seen a cash payoff for 15 years' work revert to the 49 percent share of Kal he'd always owned. True, the company was a lot bigger than it had been in 1953, but Jim also had significantly fewer years in which to enjoy any retirement. His early retirement plans had evaporated.

The alternative to the buyout, unveiled a few days later, re-energized Tom but didn't particularly buoy Jim's spirits. Tom saw opportunity in the growth of mining in B.C. and wanted to expand Kal's earthmover tire business to stay apace. To start with, he envisioned a new retread plant in Kamloops that had a $600,000 price tag. "My whole thought process had changed," says Tom in explaining his quick recovery from the Uniroyal debacle. "Now my thinking was long-term. I was 48, but age never entered my mind. I went ahead like I was going to live forever. If I wasn't going to sell the company, I figured I might as well build it."

Jim saw the Kamloops project as more debt and risk that would add another burden for Kal. He countered Tom's plans with a proposal of his own — that Tom buy him out. With the help of George Miller, Tom and Jim worked out an agreement that worked for both of them, thus ending their 15-year partnership. Tom fully understood his partner's position. That Jim asked to stay on as a salesman was evidence of the respect they continued to have for one another. Except for a few key people, Tom says, nobody even noticed that he and Jim were no longer partners. "He thought we had done a lot of bloody hard work and he'd just had enough," he says. "I had no concern about taking on this load by myself; I just charged into it again the same way I had when we started."

Of all the ramifications of the collapse of the Uniroyal sale, the one that may well have been most significant to Kal's future was its impact on Tom Foord. For five years, Tom had been distracted by the stock market, seeking an easy route to riches. A sudden market drop that battered his portfolio around the same time that Uniroyal backed out of its purchase of Kal made him wake up and look at the reality of his life. Reminded that hard work had been responsible for any success so far, Tom realized that it made sense to return to that formula. He focused on Kal with a new passion and clarity of purpose.

I had no concern about taking on this load by myself; I just charged into it again the same way I had when we started.

A MID-LIFE GAMBLE

In 1963, Tom's enthusiasm for building Kal began to waver. For 11 years he'd lived on the brink of failure, sacrificing a reasonable salary to pour profits back into the company to grow it. As his interest in Kal flagged, however, his fascination with the get-rich-quick thrill of gambling grew. For a while, poker at the Vernon Men's Club satisfied his urge. But when a friend named Frank King introduced him to penny stocks, his gambling habit turned toward the wild and woolly Vancouver Stock Exchange where he hoped to use his wits to make the money that he'd failed to generate with hard work at Kal. "I'm a sucker for venture," Tom acknowledges.

Not surprisingly, Tom and Frank failed to make the killing they'd hoped for in their first venture. In fact, they lost their investment. But once blooded in the stock market, they found the thrill irresistible. They began investing in companies, then moved on to chasing down mining properties they could buy early, hoping to cash in later when they went on the market. Using Kal's Cessna, the pair flew all over Western Canada and the U.S., scouting mines, checking out claims and attending mining meetings. Tom and Frank weren't making any money, Tom admits, "but compared to selling tires, it was fun."

These excursions were also occasionally dangerous. On one trip to Idaho, Tom got lost in a storm and had to dive low enough in 50-mile-an-hour wind conditions to check highway signs. "I finally spotted one and told Frank to read it, but in the conditions, he couldn't," Tom says. They eventually landed in a field and a farmer drove them to the nearest town, Walla Walla, Washington, where they spent the night near the local airport.

The next morning, after retrieving the plane and flying to the Walla Walla airport for fuel, Tom couldn't find Frank. "A waitress from the diner said, 'Your friend told me he's taking that plane,'" Tom laughs. "I looked over and Frank was waving to me from the door of a commercial plane. 'I want to fly where the only decision I have to make is coffee, tea or milk,' he yelled at me. In the end, I flew down to Boise alone and we both made it to the meeting at the same time."

For the next five years, investing in penny mining stocks consumed Tom. For a while, he actually made money. By 1969, he says, he was up $875,000 on his investments. But for the first time, he ignored the advice of canny George Miller, a no-nonsense accountant who knew the risks inherent in stock markets and especially the VSE, North America's shadiest stock market. He told Tom he was a fool not to sell. Tom, though, was determined to hit a million before selling his portfolio.

He never reached his goal. Within a year his stocks had tanked and he had lost his gains as well as most of his initial investment. "I think it scared the life out of him," says Archie Stroh. The man who vowed never to fail, and who was beginning to think he'd mastered the stock markets, had instead, like many before him and since, been humbled by it. "I was very good at buying," Tom laments, "but terrible at selling."

In the end, though, the debacle may have been worth the price. After the near disastrous mining detour, Tom returned to Kal Tire chastened and ready to achieve the success with his tire company that he'd thought would come through speculation. Time would validate his recommitment, and there was no bigger beneficiary than Kal. The company never looked back.

WERE
...OVER
THE BARON CALLING VICTOR YANKEE GOLF BEER SAUERKRAUT
ANY BODY OUT THERE ??
VICTOR YANKEE GOLF BEER SAUERKRAUT
CHINE GUN
GUISED AS SPEEDOMETER
RED BARON
VON T. FOORD
EMERG
EXI
RIVER

CHAPTER THREE: ROLLING OUT A BUSINESS PLAN

(THE 1970s)

LAUNCHING
THE PERPETUAL
TALENT HUNT

At first, Tom found running Kal on his own exhilarating. True, 11 years after winning the Rogers Pass contract, Kal Tire was still struggling, but at least it was an established business. When Tom completed the buyout of Jim Lochhead's 49 percent of Kal in 1972, he paid $100,000. In effect, that put a value of just $200,000 on the entire company. Although this would be the equivalent of a little more than $1 million in 2010, it still wasn't much considering that Kal was now nearly 20 years old.

But Tom did have something to build on. Kal's sales had risen from $350,000 in 1958 to $2.2 million in 1969. Its market coverage was also promising: it had two retread plants, plus an eight-store chain with outlets in Penticton, Vernon, Nakusp, Kamloops, Williams Lake, Prince George, Fort St. James and Vanderhoof.

Ironically, one reason for Kal's success, its slim management team, was beginning to be a liability. Tom Foord had virtually run the company with help from George Miller and Jim Lochhead. That had made decision making faster and easier, enabling Kal to nimbly seize opportunities or avert problems.

By 1970, however, the lack of management bench strength was threatening both the company's growth and Tom's health. "I had a foot on every base," he says. "I was overextended and ready for the nut house." Shortly after buying out Jim, the adrenalin of sole ownership wore off. Tom, then 49, heeded George Miller's warning about his health and started searching for more help.

Tom put off adding staff, he says, because he didn't want to give false hope or hire under false pretences. He couldn't pay much either, and didn't think he'd be able to find good people for the money he was offering. "As a young company desperately short of money, you can't invite the kind of people you really want," he says. "People put their future on what you and your company can do, but you have nothing to offer. Anyone who came to work for me thought I'd be broke any day, and so would they."

Of course, even if a shortage of money at Kal hadn't been an obstacle, finding someone with the experience, energy, enthusiasm and entrepreneurial instincts that had created Kal would still have been a challenge.

But that was before the faithful Jim Lochhead, now Kal's newest employee, came across the ideal candidate.

Previous page: Kal Tire rides high — two Kal employees pose for a humorous promotional shot in the 1970s.
Opposite, from top: Out back at Kal Tire's first shop in Prince George, managed by Rod Stussi, 1973. Archie Stroh joined the company in September 1970 and was the other guiding light behind the growth of Kal Tire.

ARCHIE STROH: THE START OF AN ENDURING FRIENDSHIP

On a sales call to Prince George in 1970, Jim Lochhead ran into one of Michelin's top young salesmen, Archie Stroh. Jim was so taken by the young man that he immediately phoned Tom. "There's a fellow up here you have to meet," he told him. Tom agreed to meet Archie. "While I wasn't actively out looking for someone like Archie," says Tom, "I knew from the moment I met him that he was just the kind of man I'd been waiting for."

An Albertan, Archie had gone into the tire business at 19 and spent three and a half years with Goodyear in Edmonton, then trained with Michelin in New York State. At 28, he was full of fire and ambition and itching for a change. "I had the kind of energy that never stopped," he says, "and I was going through some soul-searching of my own. Should I open a store, build a business and have total control? Or should I be part of something and help to make it bigger?"

Archie owed much of his business ethos to having grown up in modest circumstances on the prairies. It struck a chord with Tom who saw some of his own background — and indeed, some of himself — in the young man's values. "The only difference between us was that I had 22 years of business experience on him," says Tom. "Archie had the personality and drive it takes to keep a machine in motion. He had way above average intelligence, and I recognized and liked his small-town qualities."

Tom thought Archie's background particularly suited him to the small-town markets Kal served. "In a small place you're very visible," he says. "The minute you make a mistake it's in the church pew and the beer parlour. If you do a good job, the news turns up in the same places. No matter how big you get, or how far down the road you go, you have to conduct yourself like you're still living in small towns, because the past catches up with you pretty fast if you're not careful."

Tom's pitch to invite Archie to join Kal was characteristically enigmatic — a teletype message, several feet in length, that outlined the young man's future at Kal, yet oddly promised nothing. Archie, getting into the spirit of the hiring dance, responded with a hitch of his own: he wanted to join Kal as a partner. Tom wasn't entirely opposed to the idea, but the ever pragmatic George Miller didn't think Kal should make a big bet just yet on the brash young native of New Sarepta, a village near Camrose. "You haven't proved anything," he told Archie in a meeting in Vancouver. "We can't just take you at your word; you've got to show us."

Kal was taking a chance that Archie would stay interested. It wasn't as though the company was wooing him with money. The $14,000 Tom and George were offering was $2,000 less than Archie was making with Michelin. Nor was Kal inviting Archie into an attractive, modern work environment. Physically, in fact, Kal had a feel of neglect. "The buildings were old and somewhat in disarray, because Tom had been busy with mining and the stock market," Archie says.

What Kal had that nobody else did, though, was Tom Foord. In September 1970, five months after he'd first met Jim Lochhead, Archie joined Kal. "In the end I made my decision based on my assessment of Tom and his character," he says. "And Tom's character is impeccable."

Archie joined a team that included Colin Campbell, Jack Kristensen and Tom — plus Kal's *éminence grise*, George Miller. Colin Campbell in particular was

KAL TIRE COMMENCED OPERATI
HAD STEADY GROWTH THROUGH THE P
1970 KELLY RICHARDSON WITH BRAN
HOOF AND FORT ST JAMES WAS ACQU
I WAS PLANNING THE BAND LUG PLA
THIS COMMENCED OPERATIONS IN EA
EXPANSION OF THE ABOVE TWO OPER
TO KEEP IN TOUCH AND CONTROL TH
VARIOUS LOCATIONS. HOWEVER, IT
TIME THAT THE EXPANSION NOW REQ
THE ORGANIZATION TO ASSIST ME A
YOU HAVE THE KNOWLEDGE OF THE I
MY PLANS.

IN AN ORGANIZATION OF OUR
DEFINE SPECIFICALLY THE SCOPE O
FROM FAIRLY MENIAL TASKS TO OTH
CLUDING DEALING WITH THE EMPLOY
HOWEVER, TO GIVE YOU A GENERAL
I DETAIL BELOW SOME SPECIFIC AR
ATTENTION AND OHTERS THAT WOULD
CARRYING OUT THIS WORK YOU WOUL
HEADQUARTERS AND WORKING DIRECTI
NECESSARY TO GET THE JOB DONE.

SOME OF THE FIRST AREAS I

IN THE YEAR -1953-- AND HAS

OD TO 1969. IN THE YEAR

S AT PRINCE GEORGE, VANDER-

ED AND DURING THE SAME PERIOD

IN KAMLOOPS, AND AS YOU KNOW

1971. PRIOR TO THE

ONS IT WAS NOT POSSIBLE FOR ME

OPERATING FUNCTIONS AT THE

AS BEEN EVIDENT TO ME FOR SOME

RES THAT OTHERS BE TAKEN INTO

THE MANAGEMENT LEVEL. I BELIEVE

ISTRY AND THE ENERGY TO FIT INTO

E IT IS ALWAYS DIFFICULT TO

ANYONE'S ACTIVITIES, IT RANGES

OF GREAT IMPORTANCE, IN-

AND OUR CUSTOMKS, ETC.

A OF WHAT I HAVE IN MIND

THAT NEED IMMEDIATE

ON A CONTINUING BASIS. IN

E OPERATING FROM OUR VERNON

WITH ME WITH THE AUTHORITY

LD INTEND PUTTING YOUR KNOW-

MAKING GOOD ON A MISHAP

In 1972, Jim Lochhead began calling on Lyle Kennedy who handled supplies — including tires — at a field site for Dillingham Construction. Lyle repeatedly rebuffed him, but Jim kept returning week after week, making his pitch. "He just wouldn't leave me alone," says Lyle. "Finally I said, okay, let's give it a try."

Lyle gave Jim an order to transport a trailer full of tires for retreading at Kal's Kamloops plant. Jim made arrangements to pick them up. But before the job was done, the Thompson River, which ran behind the retread plant, rose above its levees and the pile of tires floated away in the flood. An embarrassed Jim was forced to call Lyle to explain the situation. "We're not starting out on a very good footing," Lyle dryly pointed out.

Luckily he agreed to give Jim a chance to rectify the situation. A week later, Jim arrived at Lyle's yard with a trailer-load of retreaded tires to replace the ones that had drifted away.

The gesture and its promptness impressed Lyle, and Dillingham contracted Kal for its tire needs for the next decade. During that time, Lyle came to appreciate Kal's approach to doing business, so much so that in 1982 he accepted a position with the company.

pleased by Archie's arrival. He regarded it as further evidence that Tom was truly reinvigorated after what Colin considered five years in the stock-market wilderness. "During that time, the business had just sat there," says Archie. "Colin's attitude was 'Now at last we can get back to selling tires.'"

Archie still remembers Tom's words on Archie's first day at work: "He told me, 'I'll never thank you.' True to his word, for the next 35 years he never did. But he also never criticized me. Together we built this tremendous trust between us. If I made a mistake we'd talk about it, but not in any critical fashion."

Indeed, Archie recalls Tom defending him in partners' meetings after Archie had made a number of mistakes. "Tom quietly pointed out that it was understandable that I made more mistakes than others because I made more decisions," he says. "He trusted me to go out and look for opportunities and find the right people and build the business. And I made sure that trust was never violated."

Once Archie was in harness, he and Tom aggressively went to work growing Kal. With Tom in the pilot's seat, they spent hundreds of hours flying around the B.C. Interior, visiting existing stores and scouting for new ones. "As a grassroots team you couldn't beat us," says Tom. Practices that they developed on their trips and that worked well became part of their standard operating procedure — and eventually Kal's.

Tom, for instance, always insisted on going to the back shop of a store first, to shake the hands of the men working on tires. The shop-first approach had nothing to do with spying on the manager. "Tom doesn't think that way," says Archie. "We did it because if we started with the manager and got tied up there, we'd never get to the shop. We didn't want that to happen. The boys in the shop appreciate it when you spend time with them. That's where the loyalty to Kal begins."

Eventually, as Kal covered a wider swath of the Canadian west, Archie also got his pilot's licence, the better to visit mining and logging customers' sites and Kal's stores. When negotiating to buy new locations, however, he preferred getting around by car. Seeing the countryside at ground level, he says, gave him a better feel for the marketplace Kal was considering getting into.

Archie was careful never to violate Tom's trust in his judgment. But his headstrong impatience saw him occasionally stretch its limits. Once, early in their business relationship, Tom approved his request to replace Kal Tire's decrepit little store in Williams Lake. But he hadn't known precisely what Archie had in mind. "I bought a bottling depot warehouse for $110,000 — a lot of money in those days," Archie says. "Then I spent another $80,000 fixing it up. I was never much on due diligence or details but the fact that he trusted me with that much money made me a far more diligent person."

Tom and Archie continued adding locations wherever their existing or potential customers were, especially in prime logging areas around the towns of Clearwater, Mackenzie, Grand Forks and Princeton

TAKING A CHANCE ON COLIN

Tom's ability to overlook flaws when he saw potential in someone was tested when he met Colin Campbell. Colin had been a customer of Tom's at his service station in the 1950s. Two years younger than Tom, Colin was a travelling salesman for a tobacco company and battled a drinking problem. Tom admits that he had plenty of reasons to dismiss Colin's interest in coming to work for him. And yet, he liked Colin and recognized his intelligence and loyalty.

A few years after founding Kal, when he and Jim were considering a Kamloops branch, Tom took a chance on Colin by offering him a conditional deal: if he quit drinking, Tom would give him a 20 percent interest in the Kamloops outlet. Colin agreed to the deal, and repaid Tom's faith in him. He quit drinking, made the Kamloops store profitable and continued to be one of Kal's most loyal employees.

Ironically, there came a time when Colin's faith in Tom was tested — by Tom's stock-market adventures. Colin had come to love Kal, but he worried that Tom was becoming distracted and ignoring the company. When Colin heard of the plans to invest in the Kamloops retread plant, he couldn't have been more pleased. It was a sign that Tom was becoming engaged again.

in B.C.'s forested interior. Financing for expansion generally came from cash flow. The policy of sinking profits into Kal didn't do much for the partners' personal bank accounts; they suffered low pay in the short term, hoping that their shares in Kal would be worth more in the long term.

Spending to create new outlets didn't leave much for upgrading those that Kal already owned, few of which could be described as palatial. It also meant the company was usually short of cash and an unexpected capital expense would compound the shortage. Kal had no choice, for instance, but to replace the Nakusp branch store; the one they opened in 1954 fell into a sinkhole. And when the original Vernon store became an embarrassment, they tore it down and built one on a better site in Kal's hometown.

RICHARD HAMILTON'S WORLD OF MULTI-TASKING

By 1973 it was apparent to Tom that Kal's growth was still outstripping management's ability to cope. Tom and Archie believed that Richard Hamilton, who had a marketing background with Hudson's Bay Company and who had moved back to Vernon, would be an ideal hire. George Miller, though, believed Kal's first requirement was a credit manager. Tom's compromise was to hire Richard, but start him out as credit manager.

As it turned out, Richard showed an aptitude for financial management. He followed that job with a term as supervisor of seven or eight stores for a few years. When Kal established itself sufficiently in retail markets to warrant a full-time marketing manager, Richard finally stepped into the role he'd been trained for. But even that appointment had a Kal-like quirk. "We also put him in charge of purchasing," Archie says. "We figured the guy who was trying to move inventory out the door should have a good feel for what was coming in. It turned out to be a great idea."

Since inventory had to be transported, Tom and Archie put Richard in charge of Kal's supply chain as well. At first, the job mainly involved scheduling Kal's single truck on a once-a-week tire delivery to the company's stores, but by 1981 the growing number of stores, with too much distance between them, began bogging down deliveries. Kal rose to the challenge by expanding its fleet to four vehicles and by outsourcing its trucking through an affiliation with Bert Sauer Trucking, a Kamloops-based firm that has handled Kal's transportation ever since.

By the time he finally had an opportunity to put his marketing background to work, Richard had been in enough positions to have absorbed how Kal operated. But it didn't make his job much easier. "Advertising tires is tough, because they aren't an impulse buy," he says. "People don't buy tires and store them until they need them, like they do with underwear or soap. If they aren't interested at the moment, they won't pay attention."

The first marketing themes he developed were Kal's first, too. The catchphrases "You will like us for more than our tires" and "Good, Better, Best" were posted in stores to encapsulate Kal's commitment to customers. "We were always trying to control our costs," says Richard, "so I didn't have much of a budget."

As businesses of all sorts collapsed in the recession of 1981, Richard adjusted Kal's message to emphasize its deep roots and staying power. The objective was to instill in customers confidence that Kal would continue to offer top-quality service despite tough economic times. But it wasn't an easy message to convey, Richard says, until he hit on the idea of using Tom Foord as the messenger. Who better exuded the feeling of consistency, service and integrity, he reasoned?

Opposite: The Nakusp branch store, which opened in 1954, nearly fell into a sinkhole around 1977. **Above:** Richard Hamilton, hired in 1973, was credit and marketing manager and all-round multi-tasker.

The idea wasn't an easy sell to Tom, though. "We had a hell of a time getting him to do commercials," says Archie. "We won him over by pointing out that he was telling customers something that he genuinely believed." Once engaged, Tom turned out to be the perfect Kal spokesman. "Later on, we got Tom to talk about our programs in TV commercials — programs like customer protection," Richard says. "It didn't matter whether people bought their tires in Vernon or Prince George, they would be looked after in any Kal Tire store. Tom talked about the great service and all our guarantees. He was pretty amazing, actually. He is such a sincere guy, and good-looking, so he came across very well. We shot commercials with Tom for five or six years."

It helped that Tom was promoting industry firsts introduced by Kal. He was completely comfortable pointing out how features like Kal's lifetime warranty on tires set it apart from its competitors. "Our warranties weren't supported by the rubber companies," Richard notes. "A lot of tire dealers later jumped on the bandwagon, but we were unique at the time."

Concepts Richard introduced, such as Kal's refusal to regard tires as a commodity sold on price, have since become an integral part of Kal's strategic marketing. "Tom was always looking for something that made us different," says Richard. "We let people know that we weren't the cheapest place in town, but we sure looked after them."

MAKING SENSE OF FINANCES

In Tom's mind, a business could consider itself a success when it was big enough to need — and afford — a chartered accountant on staff. George Miller was a valued business and financial consultant to Tom, but he was never on Kal's payroll. The hiring of accountant Larry Wynn in 1974 highlighted how far Kal had come in just over 20 years.

Larry began his accounting career in Vernon, then practised in Toronto and Vancouver, where he was living when Tom approached him about moving back to Vernon to work for Kal. The proposal was rather a long shot. Tom vaguely knew Larry's family; he had delivered fuel in the late 1940s to the Wynn farm in Armstrong, 15 miles north of Vernon, but that was before Larry was even born. When he met Tom and George Miller in Vancouver to discuss working for Kal, Larry didn't know much about the business. By the time he left the meeting, he was so impressed by Tom and the Kal story that he terminated his existing employment contract and signed on as Kal's chief financial officer.

Larry's first assignment was more filing than accounting. While focusing on growth, Kal's record keeping hadn't evolved much above stuffing receipts into a box. It had taken tentative steps to automate by having an outside firm process its accounts receivable electronically, but it lacked the technology to deal with the electronic results the firm generated.

Larry patiently recorded all the receipt information. He then wrote a computer program that could handle electronic accounting and create proper balance sheets and cash flow statements. Once he had a better picture, though, he wasn't sure he liked what he saw. The $600,000 capital expense commitment Tom had made for the Kamloops retread plant, he recognized, would eventually earn a good return on investment. But it left Kal cash-strapped in the short term. Larry managed to persuade the bank to lend Kal $300,000 to cover its immediate debts, but the implications of defaulting on the loan, he says, scared him.

Indeed, the process of assembling the financial statements for the bank led him to wonder exactly what he'd landed himself in at Kal, where he'd been putting in 12-hour days since arriving. "We had to include the salaries of the top five highest-paid people," he says. "When I found out that the truck driver was earning more than I was, I'm not sure I stayed until midnight that night."

BERT SAUER KEEPS TRUCKING

Bert Sauer, owner of a small Kamloops trucking company, started doing business with Kal Tire in 1981 when Archie Stroh and Richard Hamilton asked if he could handle Kal's transportation needs. At the time Bert had just three tractor units, and Kal's stores were concentrated in the B.C. Interior, from the Okanagan Valley, north to Prince George, Watson Lake and Grand Forks, and west to Terrace. Sitting down with a map, Bert calculated the logistical requirements of the Kal outlets in their different locations, and then plotted efficient routes and delivery frequencies.

Bert soon found his resources strained. "Nobody could have ever predicted how big Kal would get," he says. "And as we kept growing, we had to expand our fleet too."

For contractors like Bert, there are risks in taking on the capital expense to grow to serve a dominant customer. If the customer's business sours, so do the contractor's revenues, but payments on his equipment continue.

That was not the case for Kal Tire and Bert Sauer Trucking. By 2010, Bert had enjoyed an almost 30-year relationship with Kal. "We started out with three tractors, but now we have 48. We also have 190 pup trailers, five super-B train trailer units, 48 dolly converters for handling tires, eight short, flat-decks and twenty 45-foot vans."

Bert Sauer Trucking now covers the transportation needs of Kal Tire for every province in which Kal has a presence. "We put in over three million miles a year," Bert says. "We've gotten used to Kal's growth and in response have done a lot of our own."

Opposite: CFO Larry Wynn joined Kal Tire in 1974 after a meeting with Tom and George Miller in Vancouver. **Above, from left:** Huge off-the-road trucks at a Kal-serviced mine site. Bert Sauer, whose vehicles built up Kal transport.

Like most Kal employees, Larry enjoyed the freedom to do his job without interference. The only disagreement he had with Tom in 26 years at Kal, he says, came when he reported the value of two new trucks on the financial statements. Tom, who hated being surprised by bad news, was upset that the trucks, still unused by Kal, were valued at 30 percent less than their cost. Larry placated him by explaining that depreciation is required by accounting standards. "But from that day on," Larry says, "I made sure I never delivered Tom a negative surprise without a fair warning it was coming."

TEAM BUILDING

Finding managerial talent was a perennial challenge for Kal but the company got a couple of breaks in the 1970s. One was the attention Kal received for being a fair employer and an increasingly dynamic place to work. Its reputation appealed to good staff who then attracted managers of a similar quality.

Bruce Cantalope was a prime example of the phenomenon. Archie Stroh had known Bruce for years as a hard-working veteran of the tire business with the sort of background Kal was looking for. He'd worked part-time delivering tires for Goodyear when he was 16 and spent three years in a tire shop as a student; when he was 23 years old, Goodyear made him its youngest Canadian manager.

Bruce was still only 30 in 1974 when Archie hired him as a partner in Kal's Vernon store which Kal ran as Vernon Tire Centre. Three years later, Tom and Archie promoted him to supervise six stores, working from Prince George where Kal was opening a new outlet. A decade after joining Kal, Bruce, a gruff workaholic, was vice-president of stores and a partner in the company.

Tom's recruiting technique usually focused more on an individual's personal qualities than his résumé. He had known Gary Morris as a youth in Vernon and got to know him better later as a fellow member of the Vernon Men's Club. Even if Gary knew nothing about tires, Tom figured, as a salesman for Finning, a Western Canadian heavy equipment dealer, he knew enough about the machines shod with Kal's tires. He hired Gary, 39 years old at the time, in 1979 as a salesman. "I knew he'd be good with construction people," he says. "And he did an excellent job for us."

He'd come to know Allan Jewell, an accountant with KPMG in Vernon who was associated with local United Way, when Allan asked Tom to be the charity's honorary chairman. Tom held the position for several years, working alongside Allan. In 1988 he invited Allan to join Kal. "He told me I'd have a lot more fun with Kal than in a public accounting practice," Allan says. "I decided to take the plunge, but on two conditions: that I would not work on the accounting side, and that I come in as a partner."

It wasn't hard for Tom to meet his conditions. "I really didn't have an accounting job for him anyway," he confesses. Instead, he assigned Allan the task of computerizing Kal's stores and warehouses, at which Allan excelled. He eventually became vice-president of purchasing and distributing and stayed at Kal for almost 20 years — none of them on the accounting side. Tom was right on the mark with his recruiting pitch, too, Allan says with a laugh: "I did have more fun than I would have as an accountant in public practice."

More impressive than Tom's unorthodox recruiting practice was his ability to attract quality people who seemed to understand Kal's culture and work ethic, and who integrated quickly, becoming part of an efficient team with a common goal. "Somehow, it all worked," agrees Archie Stroh. "We were like different spokes from different places assembled on one wheel. But we respected each other's perspectives and got a lot of things done right."

A DIVORCE
AND A PROPOSAL

Uniroyal remained Kal Tire's supplier for four years after its deal to buy the company fell through. It was an uncomfortable period for Kal. The mutual dependency that had made the relationship a success had now swung too far in Uniroyal's favour and Tom no longer felt the same allegiance to his supplier that he'd previously had.

One of his overarching business principles was to be needed. So long as Kal built a strong market presence, he'd reasoned, it would always have the respect of its supplier. But Uniroyal's about-face left him feeling vulnerable. "When Uniroyal decided to focus on the chemical side of its business and concentrate on passenger tires and make only a small investment in truck tires, they no longer needed us," he says.

For Tom it was a point of pride not to make the first conciliatory move. "I make it a rule not to go to the supplier hat in hand to ask for something," he says. "It's a lot like a poker game; if a supplier comes to you, you've got the first ace in the hole. I will go on bended knee to a customer, but never to a supplier. When I saw the shift with Uniroyal, I knew it was time to look for an alternative; the tricky part was how to go about it without looking desperate or asking for any favours."

Archie, who in four years had become Kal's de facto operations chief, kept his ear to the ground. On the basis of what he was hearing in the gossipy tire business, he had recommended to Tom that Goodyear would be a good fit for Kal. It was a leading maker of the OTR products used by miners, and OTRs accounted for an increasing slice of Kal's sales. "Tom was worried about that, though," says Archie. "He'd just been blindsided by Uniroyal and didn't trust Goodyear to be much better. I understood that too, but it was frustrating still being with Uniroyal under the circumstances."

Tom's decision to bide his time turned out to be a good tactic. He was still pondering his next move when Bob Markham, a senior vice-president of Goodyear, showed up at his office one morning. "Our conversation was brief and to the point," says Tom. "He simply said, 'Our company is the best at manufacturing a product, and you are the best in the service industry. Why don't we make a deal?'"

Archie denies having anything to do with sending Bob Markham to see Tom. But he admits he was relieved when the meeting took place. "He put to rest Tom's fears that Goodyear would threaten Kal's independence," Archie says. "He and Tom hit it off right away."

Tom admits he had trouble concealing his excitement at the hand he'd suddenly been dealt. "Goodyear was a very good manufacturer of earthmover tires," he says, "and I had just made the decision to go into the earthmover tire business by building the expensive retread plant in Kamloops. So this was music to my ears."

Tom and George Miller met with Goodyear management in Vancouver to put the deal together. Pleased with Kal's prospects, and feeling needed once more, Tom, ever the poker player, couldn't resist some bluffing to sweeten the pot. His hole card was the knowledge that Brad Ragan, the retread executive from Georgia with whom he'd done business, headed a public company. That meant he had to disclose to securities' regulators things such as his company's arrangements with suppliers, and Tom thought that kind of information would be good to know.

Sure enough, Brad's regulatory filings showed that his company had an inventory-financing arrangement with Goodyear, based on the rate of inventory turnover. Tom figured Kal was bringing enough to the table in its partnership with Goodyear that it should be eligible for a financing deal,

Opposite, from top: Bruce Cantalope at 23 was Goodyear's youngest Canadian manager and was hired in 1974 to work in Kal's Vernon store — he went on to become VP of stores and a partner in the company. Gary Morris, hired in 1979 even though he knew little about tires, turned out to be a superb salesman. Allan Jewell, who came on in 1988 to computerize Kal's stores and warehouses, eventually became VP of purchasing and distribution and stayed with the company for nearly 20 years. **Above:** Kal Tire and Goodyear signage being shipped to outlets — Tom Foord sealed the deal with Goodyear in 1973.

THE WORLD'S UGLIEST TIRES

In their search to do things better, Tom and Archie looked into every new retreading idea that might make the Kal retread plants in Kamloops and Prince George more efficient. They hit pay dirt when they came across a process developed by Bandag, a U.S. company founded by Roy Carver.

Roy had acquired rights to a German retreading process, had refined it in his Muscatine, Iowa, plant and was selling franchises. Instead of using hot steam kettles as in conventional retreading, the Bandag process used rubber that was already vulcanized, which enabled the tires to be cured at cooler temperatures. A belt strapped around the casing with a band held it together and was stapled onto the tire.

Tom and Archie were in agreement about one aspect of Bandag retreads: they were ugly compared to conventional recaps. "There was a clearly defined line between the old and the shiny new rubber," Archie says. "It was like a woman who'd applied makeup to half of each cheek. And because the result was so ugly, the Bandag process was practically laughed out of the industry."

Manufacturers also had little confidence in Bandag retreads, dismissing the notion that they would compete with new-tire sales. Tom and Archie, though, knew not only tires, but also the tire business. And they understood the economic importance of retreads to their customers.

They saw efficiency in the fact that the Bandag technique permitted tire casings to be reused. "We realized from the moment we met Roy Carver that he had a phenomenal process," Archie says. "It was almost as if the tires never wore out. We knew we could sell that service to our customers." Kal Tire became one of Canada's first Bandag franchisees in Canada in 1972. In 1974 it added another Bandag plant when it bought Mainland Bandag, a Kamloops retreading plant.

Although the process revolutionized the retread business, it took 20 years for tire manufacturers to acknowledge its value to commercial customers. "They weren't about to believe that anything good could come out of a tin-shed operation in Muscatine, Iowa," says Marty Carver, who took over Bandag when his father died in 1981.

While Marty knew retreading, he attributes much of what he learned about the tire business itself to Tom Foord. "Tom was more of a mentor to me than my own dad," says Marty. "I went to school and learned all about business, but I knew nothing about relationships. I made every mistake in the book. Then I met Tom, and I trusted him implicitly. He was always as good as his word, and if he told you something, you could take it to the bank. You didn't need a contract. You never had to worry that he was going to change his position, and you could count on his loyalty."

By 2006, tire manufacturers had faced enough competition from Bandag to change their view of the importance of the retread business; Japan's Bridgestone, one of the world's largest tire-makers, thought the business of retreading looked attractive enough that it paid US$1 billion to purchase Bandag.

Marty Carver maintains that Tom Foord's credibility contributed to Bandag's excellent reputation and to Bridgestone's interest in buying the company. "Tom always knew that it's people who make a business work," Marty says, pointing specifically to Kal's AIMS as an example. "Everybody has those slogans on the wall, but he understands it on a profound level, and that is very rare. Technology is important, but in the end, trust is the most competitive weapon you have in business."

The relationship with Bandag, begun in 1972 when Tom and Archie first recognized the value of Bandag's retreading prowess for its customers, has continued to flourish under Bridgestone. In 2009, Kal was operating 12 Bandag plants across Canada.

too. "We didn't refer to Brad Ragan," he says, "but we insisted on a similar turnover deal to his on all our products, including passenger tires."

The money involved was significant enough that the Goodyear executives had to get clearance from head office in Toronto. Gordon MacNeill, Goodyear's president, agreed to the inventory financing. "It turned out to be a fantastic deal financially for us," says Tom. "From that day on, everything went click, and fell into place. Our sales volume went straight up. Suddenly doing business wasn't an uphill battle anymore."

The fact that Gordon is a Canadian, Tom reckons, gave him a better appreciation for how Kal fit in with Goodyear's operations than an executive parachuted in from the U.S. might have. Tom and Gordon subsequently became personal friends.

But Kal didn't get everything its own way. Tom wanted exclusive rights to Goodyear products for all of B.C., but Goodyear balked. It offered to sell three stores in the Interior — Vernon, Penticton and Kamloops — and promised not to compete against Kal in those markets, a compromise that wasn't too bad for Kal. "Essentially there would be no Goodyear dealers or stores from the Alberta border to Vancouver," Tom says.

In retrospect, Tom says, it was probably just as well that Kal didn't get all Goodyear's B.C. outlets as it had wanted originally. Taking over stores meant buying hard assets — inventories and equipment — taking over leases and adding Goodyear's personnel to Kal's payroll. Adding to the Vancouver group, as well as with Goodyear's stores in the Interior, would have severely stretched Kal's financial and management resources.

More to the point, Kal would have lost the business agility that contributed to its success. "We weren't ready to take the risk of getting into the clutches of a supplier financially," Tom says. "The whole thing scared me a bit. We decided to remain independent, and not get involved in financial problems with them."

There were also some unexpected bonuses in the Goodyear transaction. Archie Stroh convinced Bruce Cantalope, a Goodyear manager, that his future was brighter at Kal than at Goodyear. Bruce became a partner in Kal's Vernon store. As well, Goodyear sent Harry Barnes, an experienced earthmover tire sales executive, to work with Kal. Harry was invaluable in helping develop Kal's mining business. "He did a wonderful job for us," says Tom. "Working with Harry, we got Lornex, which is now Highland Valley Copper, a big mine 45 miles out of Kamloops."

Despite the early concerns and adjustments in terms of market share, the relationship between Kal and Goodyear soon flourished. Prior to the deal, as a Uniroyal dealer, Kal had been earning respect for its customer service, but was frustrated by not having competitive tires to sell to miners. Japanese-owned Bridgestone had stepped into the vacuum to snare about 75 percent of the OTR market. Within three years of switching from Uniroyal to Goodyear, Kal reversed the market-share balance, stunning Bridgestone by grabbing 75 percent of the market for Goodyear.

"All the work we had done for the past 20 years was paying off," says Tom. "This was the beginning of the reshaping of Kal Tire."

All the work we had done for the past 20 years was paying off. This was the beginning of the reshaping of Kal Tire.

THE ASSOCIATES: FINDING A WAY TO FUEL GROWTH

Locating Kal outlets wherever they needed to be to best serve customers might have been a sound business axiom, but it didn't necessarily create the most orderly result. Because Kal's customers were often far from one another, so were its stores, which made servicing them inefficient. Bert Sauer's trucks often went near, or passed through, potential markets on their weekly delivery of new stock to Kal stores or picking up tires for retreading.

Opening new company outlets in underserved markets between existing ones would have at least partially solved the problem. But it would also have been prohibitively expensive and time-consuming. Moreover, finding or training managers familiar with the markets would have been next to impossible given Kal's resources.

In 1973 Kal launched an associates program to address the issue. The idea was to select the best independent tire dealers in smaller centres and persuade them to operate under the Kal Tire banner. The associate dealer would then gain access to Kal's volume discounts on tires and services such as retreading, and would benefit from Kal's advertising and promotion programs as well as its efficient distribution system. Kal got representation under its name in a new location run by an experienced tire-business entrepreneur already familiar with his market.

The inaugural associate program was a loose arrangement that reflected Tom's aversion to detail and red tape. Associates were expected to comply with Kal's systems and to give the same high quality of service its customers got from its corporate stores. But there was no contract between associates and Kal. "It was more of a moral agreement," Tom says. "If an associate didn't get what he wanted from us, he could get out of it in 30 days."

The verbal agreement evolved into a one-page document, and eventually into its current 40 pages. But the principles outlining the associates' relationship with Kal remained much as they had begun. Archie even insisted on retaining the 30-day cancellation clause. The thinking was, he says, "If it isn't good for both of us, let's call it off. We didn't want to handcuff anybody."

Associates' investment, relatively small in early years, has gradually increased. It is spent mainly on bringing physical aspects of associates' outlets up to the standards of corporate stores. Archie makes no apologies for the cost; associates, he argues, can more than recoup the amount from higher business volumes as a result of their association with Kal. "It was critical that the associates live by our rules so we could reflect the best of each other," he says. "And there's a by-product of the trusting relationship the associates built with us. We're an exit strategy for them. They have somebody to sell the business to when they want to retire."

Even as the associate program became more structured, independent operators recognized the merits of signing on — and the risks in not doing so. "Dealers were soon looking at us as a company to be reckoned with," says Tom. "We were expanding, and capable of coming into a town and becoming their competitor." Kal, he adds, seldom did so aggressively. "We've always treated our competition with respect."

Kal's first associate was Jim Checkley, who ran Cedarland Tire in Terrace, on the Skeena River in northwest B.C. Jim perfectly fit the profile of the associate Kal had in mind. A long-time

Terrace resident, Jim participated in the community and the local logging industry association. "We didn't take them on just to get more volume," Archie says of the associates Kal signed up. "We took on guys like Jim Checkley whose customers loved him. The market loved him, and when he became part of us, Kal Tire was also loved."

Thirty-six years later, Cedarland is still a Kal associate store, now run by Jim Checkley Jr., who took the business over from his father. Tom admits that not all associate arrangements have been as smooth. "The associates are independent birds," he says. "Sometimes it's been hard for them to switch over to our way of doing things and not to be able to do exactly what they want. But they're usually grateful for the opportunity to be an associate with an expanding company."

Kal had done a great job of setting up the associate program, but its best move may have been hiring Lloyd Higginson to oversee it. A former president of Fountain Tire, an Edmonton-based chain, Lloyd been retired for five years when Tom invited him to join Kal. From Kal's perspective, Lloyd's background uniquely qualified him to identify prospective associates as he toured the West. But he also earned the associates' respect by fiercely representing them and making sure their concerns and requests were heard in Vernon. When Lloyd died of leukemia in 2008, the associates lost a tireless advocate, and Kal lost a valued manager whose legacy is a smoothly functioning associate program.

THE MINING TIRE TEAM GOES PROSPECTING

Kal's OTR business had been primarily in the forestry sector in B.C., but it had also had its eye on mining, the province's other resource-based industry. In 1968 it took an interest in Copper Tire. The company, based in Merritt, had a small OTR repair plant that serviced gold, silver and copper mines in the area, a three-hour drive west of Vernon.

Shortly after Kal invested in Copper Tire, however, mining hit one of its typical downdrafts. High taxes and low global commodity prices conspired to demonstrate yet again the volatility of the mining sector and its risks for tire companies. Service and supply contracts that had looked excellent when signed became liabilities when mines suddenly became uneconomic and shut down, leaving tire contractors with significant costs to swallow.

In 1973, when mining started to show signs of recovery, Kal was well positioned to take advantage of the change in circumstances. It had just become a Goodyear dealer, and it had an excellent line of OTR tires to sell. Archie had also beefed up Kal's mining division. Over a period of 20 years he hired Joe Peshko to lead the group, then added Flemming Sorensen and George Frame to fill out the sales team. All three had experience in OTR products and extensive contacts in the mining industry. They were also keen to start doing some prospecting.

Over the next year or so, however, it was dawning on Archie that mining may have heated up a little too much in the Kamloops and Prince George areas. In mining, the practice of scooping the most easily recovered material first is called high-grading. Archie felt the Kamloops and Prince George stores were also high-grading after a fashion: they had contracts with miners that were profitable enough that the store managers could neglect their mainstay commercial and retail businesses and still post outstanding sales numbers.

DOING A DEAL ON A PAPER NAPKIN

Tom Foord is the first to admit that he's not always the most organized record keeper, and that his indifference toward paperwork has occasionally come back to haunt him. But it's also worked to his advantage, too, as when he did his first deal with Brad Ragan.

Brad, a towering, cigar-smoking American from Georgia, and a former employee of Goodyear, started a business retreading earthmover tires. Brad set up a meeting with Tom, hoping to interest Kal in using his patented process.

At the time, Kal used a conventional retread technique that used a mould with the tire pattern pressed into it. When uncured rubber was placed in the mould holding the tire casing and pressure was applied, the tread was imbedded in the rubber and attached to the tire casing. The drawback of the process was the capital cost of the equipment, which cost hundreds of thousands of dollars.

Brad had patented a competing retreading process called "band lug," which involved using hand tools to attach lugs that created the tread pattern on the tire casing. It was more labour-intensive than the mould-cure method, and the band lug result didn't look as neat as the tires the Kal retread plant produced.

But appearance doesn't matter on earthmoving equipment, and the band lug technique had a huge advantage over moulding: it didn't require the capital expenditure that a mould process did. Intrigued by band lug's potential, Tom and George Miller met Brad in Toronto to discuss becoming a franchisee and purchasing the necessary band lug equipment.

Tom, who was irresistibly drawn to unique individuals, still remembers their first encounter. "Brad was a real character. He was tall, a couple of years older than me and had a thick Southern accent. He constantly smoked cigars and didn't seem to be bothered a bit that the ashes were always falling onto his suit."

Brad wrote on a paper napkin a list of equipment Kal Tire would need. His itemization included two builders at $35,000 each, and a $40,000 buffer that cleaned up casings before putting treads on them. He also tacked on $1,000 for delivery — 25 cents a mile for the 4,000-mile journey from Georgia to Kamloops, B.C.

After both parties signed the napkin, Tom and George left the meeting under the impression that Brad had granted Kal Tire exclusive rights in B.C. to the patented retreading process. While the napkin document was legally binding, Brad had agreed to send a more formal contract to Tom to sign a few weeks later.

When it arrived, Tom noticed that Brad had made no mention of exclusive B.C. rights. Ignoring the oversight, he put the contract in a desk drawer and more or less forgot about it. "I was never high on signing agreements," he says. "I'm quite satisfied to do business on an honour basis."

A few years later, Tom had reason to haul the agreement out and re-read it. Brad had opened an office in Edmonton from which he hoped to sell retreading services using the band lug process. But when his salesman called on one of Kal's customers in Vancouver, Tom accused Brad of violating Kal's band lug exclusivity in B.C. Brad countered that there was nothing about exclusive rights in the contract he'd sent. "And you signed it," he told Tom.

"When I told him I hadn't, there was a stunned silence," says Tom. "I told him to look in his files. That was the last meeting we ever had. We kept on using his band lug process, with no more interference from Brad."

2x builders $35,0...
$40,000 casing buffe...
$1,000 for delivery (25 cen...

Extruding rubber at a retread plant. Kal Tire has taken two approaches to retreading — the more traditional method, which used a mould with the tire pattern pressed into it, and Brad Ragan's innovative "band lug" approach which used hand tools to attach lugs that created the tread pattern on the tire casing.

Naturally, Archie had no problem with the good sales figures. But if the mining contracts blew up — a real possibility given the industry's cyclical nature — he feared Kal wouldn't have a fallback position. The steadier bread-and-butter business that would have cushioned the loss somewhat would have migrated to other tire dealers.

Tom and Archie decided to eliminate the risk. In 1975, they set up the mining group as a stand-alone division at Kal. As part of the restructuring, Kal moved all the OTR business out of the hands of individual store managers and under the aegis of the new mining group.

The move effectively resolved the Kamloops and Prince George issue. And although Tom and Archie didn't realize it at the time, marshalling Kal's forces into a mining division was a seminal moment in Kal's history. The group would ultimately become the vehicle that carried Kal around the world as a truly multinational force in the OTR industry, with operations on five continents.

KAL STAKES ITS CLAIM

Kal's timing in pushing into mining proved propitious in one respect. The mid-1970s were marked by increased mining activity all over B.C. Unfortunately, Kal's team arrived a little late for the party. Joe Peshko, and later Flemming and George, typically spent their weeks criss-crossing the province to visit mine sites. When Joe visited a mine site to give Kal's pitch he would often discover that Crown Tire out of Edmonton and Vancouver-based Columbia Tire already had most of the business tied up.

Undeterred, they continued to stump the Interior, seeking to establish relationships with mine managers. Kal's differentiator, they made clear, was that it delivered what it promised. Their refusal to compromise their standards was not a universal scruple in the tire trade. "We made sure our customers knew we were above-board on everything," says Joe. "We gave them guarantees of our products and services, and especially delivery. Getting the right tires delivered on time is more crucial on the mining side than anywhere else."

In addition to being veterans of the OTR marketing wars, Kal's team members proved to be students of the mining industry and respected the people they dealt with. "The mining guys were friendly, straightforward and down-to-earth, and you always knew exactly where you stood with them," says Joe. "When you called on a mine, you knew what they needed, you quoted a price, they either said yes or no, and you got it all done, right then and there."

Gradually, Kal demonstrated that its claim to offer industry-leading service wasn't made idly. It began winning contracts largely on the basis of sound tire advice, efficient repair services and superior record keeping that assisted customers in extending the life of their tires. Kal also maintained an ethical high-ground. Contractors who treated all customers equally, for instance, were few and far between in the mining industry. But Kal made it a priority.

Archie recalls Kal sticking to its guns when a major customer wanted a lower price for tires because it was sure Kal was giving a competing mine a better deal. As it happened, the complaining customer took over the mine it thought Kal was favouring. "After it took a look at the acquisition's books, an executive from the acquiring company called me to apologize," says Archie. "He said, 'Boys, you were treating us right after all.' It was rewarding to hear it."

By the close of the 1970s, Kal's power play on the mining sector was paying off. The industry accounted for a significant slice of Kal's overall sales, and Archie saw it growing even more. "It's incredibly difficult to get moving from a position of standing still," he says. "But once the wheel has a little motion, it's easy to put your shoulder to it and move it right along."

As usual, it was Kal's service that earned it points with miners. Tires were one of miners' biggest operating costs after labour. Kal's strategy was to save customers money any way it could, going as far as to set up on customer's sites with its own people for mounting and dismounting tires, repair work, air checks and fleet tire inspections.

GUARANTEEING THE PRODUCT

Kal attracted attention in mining camps with its willingness to innovate when it introduced an industry-first warranty that covered its tires on customers' equipment for a specific number of operating hours. The program had the potential to be expensive if the frequency of tire failures increased. The cost of OTR mining tires at the time could be prohibitive. Even Goodyear, Kal's supplier, was dubious about guaranteeing a product that was so exposed to damage through hard use.

Kal, however, found a way to mitigate its risk and at the same time save customers money. The company set up a system for monitoring every aspect of tire usage at a mine site, from inflation-pressure to road conditions. It then delivered comprehensive reports to its customer, indicating how better maintenance could increase tires' life cycle and reduce downtime.

When customers agreed to improve, Kal assisted them. Overloading trucks, for instance, was a major cause of tire damage. Kal recognized that customers wanted to maximize operations but, as its mining team pointed out, this was false economy if tires blew. Not only was replacement expensive, so was downtime while the tire was being changed.

The kicker was that Kal augmented the business advice with technology to help customers help themselves. It borrowed scales from Goodyear and installed them over a 40-foot-long trench with concrete pads at each end. The scales, capable of handling up to 700 tons, enabled customers to monitor load weights for maximum tire wear.

Kal's innovative problem solving — it was the first to offer weighing services at mines — didn't go unnoticed in mining circles. When Occidental Petroleum, a Los Angeles company run by the legendary industrialist Armand Hammer, ran into difficulties dealing with tires at a coal mine it was developing in China, the company asked Tom for help. Tom dispatched Joe Peshko and Goodyear's tire man Harry Barnes to help train the Chinese workers. A year later, they made a return trip.

The export of Kal talent was the company's first foray into foreign markets. Thirty years later it would become a major part of the company's growth into a multinational power in the tire business.

DEBT COLLECTING ADVENTURES

Kal was not without its own challenges in the late 1970s. A chronic shortage of good managers was exacerbated by expansion and inconvenient timing. At the same time that its mining business was surging, so was its more conventional commercial segment.

By 1979 Kal had 15 outlets in B.C.'s Interior and sales of $50 million. Furthermore, as its profile rose, the popularity of its associate program was generating queries from other locations. But it all had to be administered, so Tom once more went into recruiting mode to come up with yet another winner. Robert Kehler was 23 years old and working at York Tire in Winnipeg when he answered Kal Tire's

He [Tom] said he wouldn't expect me to do something he wasn't prepared to do himself. While he worked, I just stood there chatting with him. He made me feel as if we'd known each other for years.

SWEPT AWAY BY TOM

When Don Knox joined Kal Tire in 1972, tires still came from Eastern Canada by train. One of Don's duties at Kal Tire's Vernon warehouse was unloading and stacking the tires.

The work could be dangerous. But Don's biggest fear wasn't wrestling the huge OTR tires around the four-storey building. It was the worry that he'd run into Tom Foord, Kal's founder and president. "I'd never met him," Don says. "But people talked about him as if he were some kind of god. I was nervous about how I'd react if he happened to show up."

He found out one afternoon near closing time. Don was sweeping the floor when Tom Foord dropped into the warehouse. Don reacted exactly as he'd hoped he wouldn't: he began to quake and sweat.

Tom, however, acted exactly as usual. Looking around, he casually addressed Don by name, as though they'd already met and were friends. "Then he reached into a cupboard, put on some coveralls," Don says. "I still hadn't said a word. But he took the broom from me and said, 'Here, I'll do that,' and calmly started to sweep the floor."

"I'll never forget that day," Don says. "Tom just shrugged when I told him he was doing my job. He said he wouldn't expect me to do something he wasn't prepared to do himself. While he worked, I just stood there chatting with him. He made me feel as if we'd known each other for years."

Don, who stills works for Kal on the order desk 36 years later, says he owes much of his loyalty to that incident. "I'm not sure it would happen at most companies that I know of," he says. "But from that point on, the day I met Tom Foord, I felt as though I owned a piece of Kal."

newspaper ad in 1979. He admits he wasn't exactly career planning. "I just wanted to go someplace else and do something different," he says.

The first few weeks after Tom hired him weren't exactly what Robert had in mind. He started off driving a truck for a while. Archie regarded Robert as a diamond in the rough and assigned him to work with Colin Campbell. But Kal's management needs were urgent enough that Archie cut his initiation period to a mere two weeks and posted him to fill a management vacancy at Kal's Merritt outlet.

The Merritt store was a decided challenge. Situated in the heart of logging and ranching territory in the Interior, its operations had a frontier flavour that reflected the local geography. It was also losing money. Robert, who lacks neither self-confidence nor grit, saw himself as the sheriff sent in to bring order out of chaos. "Our store was a hole in the wall, stocked with as many tires as we could handle with our one broken-down service truck," he recalls. "I was in charge of everything: managing the store, changing tires, selling tires and making sales calls to bring in business."

One of the trickiest tasks he faced was collecting the delinquent accounts that were partly responsible for the store's red ink. The Merritt store's customers weren't always in a mood to negotiate. When one defaulting customer chased him off with a shotgun, Robert resorted to taking payment in kind. He returned later and swiped a pile of railway ties he'd seen piled up behind the customer's shop. "The ties were eight feet long," he says. "It was a heck of a job loading them into the truck by myself, praying all the time I wouldn't get shot. Eventually we sold them two at a time to people who used them for landscaping."

Robert also sold a truck repossessed from the same customer. "Altogether this guy owed $2,500," he says. "But between the truck and the railroad ties we came close to cleaning up his arrears. Sometimes it sure felt like it was Wild West days. You had to be thick-skinned to make it."

In addition to performing the manual labour in the Merritt store's shop, Robert was acquiring actual management experience on the fly. "I remember getting my first statement and seeing this big red number at the bottom of the page and asking, 'Is that a loss? We lost that much?' and wondering if I'd have a job next week."

Reigning in his aggressiveness, he learned through trial and error how to make sales pitches. A natural affinity for the local logging fraternity helped him develop relationships in the business locally. He determined that the market dictated tire prices, but that customers would pay extra for good service. "We worked hard day and night," he says, "and slowly we got the margins up to where we could make a buck. When I left Merritt two and a half years later, we were making money."

By most measures, Kal had come through the 1970s in good shape. Sales in the decade had soared from $2.2 million to $50 million. Even so, Tom Foord and Archie Stroh, respectively Kal's visionary and his hard-driving lieutenant, used to carry on a bantering argument over the best way to describe the decade from Kal's point of view. To Tom the decade was "a great expansionary time." Archie, though, laughs at that. In his memory, "Helter-skelter comes to mind."

Robert Kehler's experience in Merritt did reveal a shortfall at Kal: the company lacked the structures, procedures and controls to squeeze efficiency and profitability from the store openings, and from contracts with logging, mining, trucking and construction industries companies in B.C.'s Interior.

Within a year, Tom would make personnel decisions that would go a long way toward resolving the problem for years to come.

Chuck Makowka and Tom Foord at the Victoria Steet store opening in Kamloops, circa early 1980s.

CHAPTER FOUR:
SLUGGING IT OUT IN A RECESSION

(THE EARLY 1980s)

> When everything is sliding and you can do it right, you learn how to manage your business properly. It was the best thing that could have happened to us. "

BRINGING IN KEN

Tom had never been particularly comfortable with the idea of hiring family members. So he hadn't. It wasn't so much that he disliked his relatives. On the contrary, he liked them too much and feared that becoming involved in a business arrangement had the potential to create discord.

Sticking to his self-imposed embargo wasn't always easy. He'd recognized for some time that Ken Finch would be a welcome addition to Kal's management team — except that Ken was married to Tom's eldest daughter, Jean. At 35 years old, Ken was chief engineer at Permasteel, a Vancouver engineering and construction firm, and had an opportunity to buy into the firm. When Ken approached Tom to back him in a bank loan he was taking out to buy the partnership, Tom broke one of his own rules. Instead of buying into Permasteel, he asked his son-in-law, why didn't he consider joining Kal?

Tom was careful not to oversell the job. The $24,000 or so Ken could expect at Kal was significantly less than the $65,000 he was earning at Permasteel. Apart from the pay cut, Ken also wondered how much he'd miss working on finite projects that ended in a tangible result he could point to as something he helped create. "My concern about the tire business was that there was no start and no end," Ken says. "It just keeps going on and on, and where does the satisfaction come from?"

Kal, though, became an appealing opportunity when Ken considered it from another perspective. "I'd found the whole idea frightening until I suddenly understood that Kal Tire wasn't just a tire business, it was all about people," Ken says. "Once I thought of it that way, it made it a lot easier to make the decision to take the job." In October 1980, six months after Tom broke his rule and offered him a job, Ken accepted.

A condition of Ken's acceptance was that he would eventually become a partner. Tom had no problem with that, but was adamant that his newest employee had to take a crash course in the gritty end of the tire business. Ken went to work at Kal's Lumby store, a half-hour east of Vernon, where he did everything from busting tires in the shop and making road-service calls to managing people and marketing.

Ken neither asked for nor received any special treatment. In fact, he hid his family connection from co-workers so he'd be regarded as just another new employee. "Some appreciated me, and some thought I wasn't very bright, but most of them were polite," he says. He, however, learned plenty about them — and developed an abiding respect for their practical skills and for how hard they worked. "Everyone in the outlet knew more than I did," he says.

Of course, it had never been in the cards that an engineer with management experience would continue on the shop floor. Within a few months, Ken moved on to supervise a group of managers. With five stores and two retread plants to oversee, the earlier shop-floor experience proved handy, if a little brief, he acknowledges. "I didn't much like supervising people in jobs I knew I didn't have the ability to do."

In his supervisory role, Ken showed a capacity for compassion similar to that which Tom had demonstrated when he'd used a job at Kal to help reform Colin Campbell. Ken recognized potential in

Brian McCaskill, a retread-machine operator in Kamloops. Though Brian had only a grade 10 education, was overweight and introverted and, Ken suspected, had a drinking problem, he was also a hard worker, fiercely loyal to Kal and eager to learn.

That Brian was well liked by his peers, despite his flaws, helped persuade Ken that his positive attributes outweighed his negatives ones. Using Brian's sense of responsibility on the job as a lever, Ken assigned him to set up a small retread operation and then watched closely. Although Brian struggled at first, within a year or so he repaid the faith Ken had shown in him. He gave up drinking and became so proficient and confident in his abilities that, in 1987, Kal saw fit to name him supervisor of all its retread plants.

Unfortunately, Brian McCaskill died of cancer in 2001. But for Ken, his case reinforced Tom Foord's belief that treating people with respect was a value worth maintaining at Kal. "Brian had no ego, and the way he supervised people inspired great loyalty to him," Ken says. "He helped a lot of people advance their careers. It was very rewarding to be able to help Brian reach his potential and be more than he ever dreamed he was capable of being."

TAKING ON VANCOUVER

By the time Ken Finch signed on at Kal, the company had been opening outlets for 27 years in small towns all over B.C. wherever forestry and mining flourished. In the early 1980s, the company was ready to cast off what Archie called its "hicks from the sticks" image and move into the bigger markets.

From a management standpoint, Kal had never in its history been better positioned for growth. The triumvirate of Tom, George Miller and Archie Stroh had been strengthened by the addition of Larry Wynn, Richard Hamilton, Bruce Cantalope, Gary Morris and Ken Finch. In addition to buying individual dealerships when opportunities arose, Kal added to its shopping list competitors who owned several stores, perhaps a warehouse and even a retread plant. For the first time, Kal had the management depth to handle the deal and integrate acquisitions.

Opposite: Ken Finch worked out a more clearly defined structure for the company after Kal Tire was hit hard by the 1980s recession. **Above, from left:** Ken Finch starts out as one of the guys — "Kal Tire wasn't just a tire business, it was all about the people." At Kal Tire retread operations, reminders about the value of customer service are never far away.

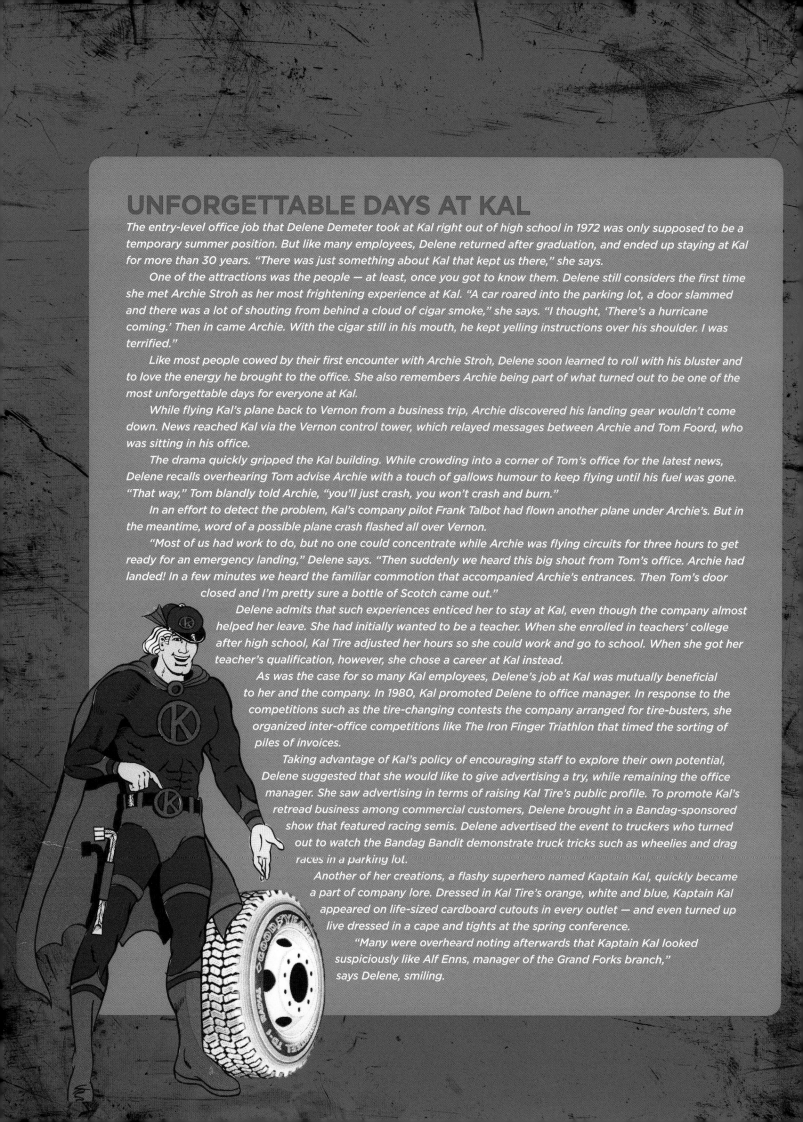

UNFORGETTABLE DAYS AT KAL

The entry-level office job that Delene Demeter took at Kal right out of high school in 1972 was only supposed to be a temporary summer position. But like many employees, Delene returned after graduation, and ended up staying at Kal for more than 30 years. "There was just something about Kal that kept us there," she says.

One of the attractions was the people — at least, once you got to know them. Delene still considers the first time she met Archie Stroh as her most frightening experience at Kal. "A car roared into the parking lot, a door slammed and there was a lot of shouting from behind a cloud of cigar smoke," she says. "I thought, 'There's a hurricane coming.' Then in came Archie. With the cigar still in his mouth, he kept yelling instructions over his shoulder. I was terrified."

Like most people cowed by their first encounter with Archie Stroh, Delene soon learned to roll with his bluster and to love the energy he brought to the office. She also remembers Archie being part of what turned out to be one of the most unforgettable days for everyone at Kal.

While flying Kal's plane back to Vernon from a business trip, Archie discovered his landing gear wouldn't come down. News reached Kal via the Vernon control tower, which relayed messages between Archie and Tom Foord, who was sitting in his office.

The drama quickly gripped the Kal building. While crowding into a corner of Tom's office for the latest news, Delene recalls overhearing Tom advise Archie with a touch of gallows humour to keep flying until his fuel was gone. "That way," Tom blandly told Archie, "you'll just crash, you won't crash and burn."

In an effort to detect the problem, Kal's company pilot Frank Talbot had flown another plane under Archie's. But in the meantime, word of a possible plane crash flashed all over Vernon.

"Most of us had work to do, but no one could concentrate while Archie was flying circuits for three hours to get ready for an emergency landing," Delene says. "Then suddenly we heard this big shout from Tom's office. Archie had landed! In a few minutes we heard the familiar commotion that accompanied Archie's entrances. Then Tom's door closed and I'm pretty sure a bottle of Scotch came out."

Delene admits that such experiences enticed her to stay at Kal, even though the company almost helped her leave. She had initially wanted to be a teacher. When she enrolled in teachers' college after high school, Kal Tire adjusted her hours so she could work and go to school. When she got her teacher's qualification, however, she chose a career at Kal instead.

As was the case for so many Kal employees, Delene's job at Kal was mutually beneficial to her and the company. In 1980, Kal promoted Delene to office manager. In response to the competitions such as the tire-changing contests the company arranged for tire-busters, she organized inter-office competitions like The Iron Finger Triathlon that timed the sorting of piles of invoices.

Taking advantage of Kal's policy of encouraging staff to explore their own potential, Delene suggested that she would like to give advertising a try, while remaining the office manager. She saw advertising in terms of raising Kal Tire's public profile. To promote Kal's retread business among commercial customers, Delene brought in a Bandag-sponsored show that featured racing semis. Delene advertised the event to truckers who turned out to watch the Bandag Bandit demonstrate truck tricks such as wheelies and drag races in a parking lot.

Another of her creations, a flashy superhero named Kaptain Kal, quickly became a part of company lore. Dressed in Kal Tire's orange, white and blue, Kaptain Kal appeared on life-sized cardboard cutouts in every outlet — and even turned up live dressed in a cape and tights at the spring conference.

"Many were overheard noting afterwards that Kaptain Kal looked suspiciously like Alf Enns, manager of the Grand Forks branch," says Delene, smiling.

As Tom and George Miller engineered deals over the years, they'd developed a rough formula to determine a purchase price. Essentially, they bought the inventory at its cost and equipment at its current assessed value, took over the store lease and kept the employees who wanted to stay. Kal avoided buying accounts receivable, but arranged to collect them. It also paid the seller a specified amount for goodwill. "But it wasn't much in the beginning," says Archie. "Frankly, there wasn't much goodwill there in some cases."

In business terms, it was a classic business strategy that consolidated a fragmented business under the wing of a single operator. The buyer — Kal — got exposure in a wide number of locations with operation by a local entrepreneur. The seller got advantages such as the buying power of a bigger organization, and centralized systems like accounting and advertising.

Of course, the seller also received money for his operation. Once the amount was agreed upon, coming up with the financing was occasionally a more difficult proposition for Kal. One source was its own profits. Management typically eschewed big salaries as Kal focused on growth, and poured profits back into the company to pay for it. But even that often didn't cover the cost of purchases. "We weren't making enough to buy places," Tom says. "We had to be creative."

One of Tom's more inspired methods of financing deals came indirectly from Kal's suppliers. In those days, if Kal could sell tires from its inventory long before it had to pay for them, it could use the money until the tire bill came due. Rather than collect interest on it in a short-term account, Tom didn't see why Kal shouldn't use it to acquire a store.

The practice was decidedly nerve-wracking. "We were always on edge working with somebody else's money," Tom acknowledges. In a worst-case situation, the invoice from the supplier for the tires Kal had already sold came due before Kal could sell enough from its new stock to pay the bill. To bridge the gap, Kal had to take on a bank loan. But then the loan had to be paid off with interest. "I think I was in business for 30 years before I got free of the bank," says Tom.

Kal's custom of dealing fairly with customers and suppliers, a hallmark of Tom Foord's business style, was a courtesy it also extended to the owners of businesses it was negotiating to buy. One reason was Tom's empathy for entrepreneurs he was dealing with. But he also knew that Kal's straight-shooting ways would burnish its reputation in the industry and make it easier to attract other potential sellers.

There was evidence that the practice worked. In the late 1970s Kal bought a store in 100 Mile House, in the Interior of B.C., from Advanx Tire, a Vancouver-based chain owned by Frank Stewart. Frank felt the deal had gone smoothly. In 1981, distracted by his growing interest in real estate, Frank decided to sell his stores on the coast and get out of the tire business. Recalling the earlier transaction, he made Kal his buyer of choice.

Advanx had five outlets plus a warehouse in the city, one store in Nanaimo on Vancouver Island, and what Tom and George regarded as a good image. But on the eve of the deal, when they were preparing to head to Vancouver to negotiate the Advanx deal, George Miller suffered a heart attack. In his stead, Tom invited Kal's chief financial officer Larry Wynn to assist him on the deal — the first he'd done without George, his loyal wingman.

Larry, acting as George's stand-in, immediately contracted a case of the jitters. "It was our move into the big smoke and I was scared as hell," he says. As it turned out, he had ample justification. Tom, supposedly the old pro, was just as nervous. When Frank Stewart offered Tom Advanx's financial statements, a standard procedure in a sales negotiation, Tom airily dismissed the gesture with a wave. "He says to Frank, 'Keep your financial statements. Just tell me your sales and we'll take it from there,'" says Larry.

It was a classic Tom Foord gambit — trust your intuition and if a deal feels right, do it. Larry was well aware that Tom had had more than his share of success following his instincts. All the same, as an accountant, and as Kal's CFO responsible for the company's financial health, Larry was horrified by his boss's cavalier gesture. The Advanx deal, he knew, would be tough enough to work out *with* the financial statements; he didn't want to contemplate the prospects of trying to do it *without* them.

Larry opted to keep his counsel until they broke for lunch. But then he quietly offered to do the talking when negotiations resumed. A visibly relieved Tom accepted in an instant. "The whole tone of the meeting changed in the afternoon," Larry remembers. "When I started talking and looking at the details, Tom could sit back, consider the big picture and comment when he wanted. We turned out to be a pretty good team."

In the course of the negotiation, Larry got a front row seat in a master class of hardball negotiating when an impasse threatened to scupper the deal. Neither Tom nor Frank indicated to Larry any sign of giving in. "They were both tough guys who'd built good businesses," he says. "During a long, dead silence, I can remember thinking 'He who speaks next, loses.' It turned out to be Frank. In short order we wrapped up the deal. We had bought Advanx."

At about $12 million, Advanx wasn't cheap. And as soon as Tom and Larry sealed the deal and left the hotel, Tom realized he'd made an error that cost Kal more than necessary. He'd forgotten to get a buy-out option on leases, which meant Kal would have to continue to rent former Advanx properties, rather than own them.

Despite the miscue, the acquisition was a watershed for Kal. It had moved out of its comfort zone of the Interior of B.C. Advanx represented its biggest expansion yet, and a move into the biggest city it had ever operated in. Unfortunately, the buyer's euphoria Kal was feeling would soon fade. Though Kal Tire didn't yet know it, it had purchased Advanx on the cusp of the deepest economic recession since the Great Depression.

An Advanx warehouse that was part of the deal would come to symbolize the recession's impact on Kal. Kal had earmarked the building, situated practically under the Port Mann Bridge between Surrey and Coquitlam in Metro Vancouver, as a potential distribution hub for further growth in the Vancouver area. But within a few months, Kal would be converting part of the building into a dormitory for its management to save money on their hotel rooms when they were in Vancouver on business.

LESSONS FROM
A RECESSION

With sales of about $50 million, Kal appeared to have momentum at the beginning of 1981. In addition to the Advanx takeover, it opened a new store in Westbank on the west side of Okanagan Lake, giving it a second location in the Kelowna area. The associate dealer program was also starting to show signs of success. New associates signed on in Prince George, Smithers, New Hazelton and Houston on Highway 16 northwest of Prince George.

Meanwhile, however, the clouds on the economic horizon continued to build and darken. Unemployment, steadily rising since 1979, was approaching 10 percent. Inflation, historically in the 3 percent range, had risen steadily to more than 9 percent in 1975, and then soared ominously to 14 percent by 1980.

Efforts by central bankers to control inflation only drove interest rates into the stratosphere. Consumers and businesses facing borrowing rates of 20 percent or more put the brakes on spending. Government over-regulation, typified by the federal National Energy Program, especially detested in the West, further dampened business activity.

Kal, like most businesses, began feeling the impact. Usually punctual corporate customers began stalling in paying their bills, and winning new tire business had become more difficult. Kal Tire occasionally had to scramble to pay its bills and cover its payroll. Somewhat puzzled by what they were seeing, Kal's gung-ho young managers responded as they always had when business seemed to be slow: they exhorted each other to put in more hours, make more sales calls and put more effort into collections.

It was an understandable response in a way. Archie Stroh, 39, was the senior member of the operating team. "Except for Tom, the rest of us had all been born after 1941," he says, "so we'd seen nothing but growth, and all of a sudden we had to deal with this animal called recession."

Tom Foord, however, was 59 at the time, and he knew first-hand the havoc that the economic upheaval from a recession could cause. He'd lived through the biggest recession of all, the Great Depression, and it had informed his personal values system. The thoughts of what anything like it might do galvanized him. He was vacationing in California when he called Archie Stroh and told him to launch a cost-cutting program.

> *It was a classic Tom Foord gambit — trust your intuition and if a deal feels right, do it.*

Above, from left: Kal Tire employees ham it up at one of the B.C. stores. Floyd Daniels (right) and another Kal Tire employee doing an alignment at the Prince George store.

83

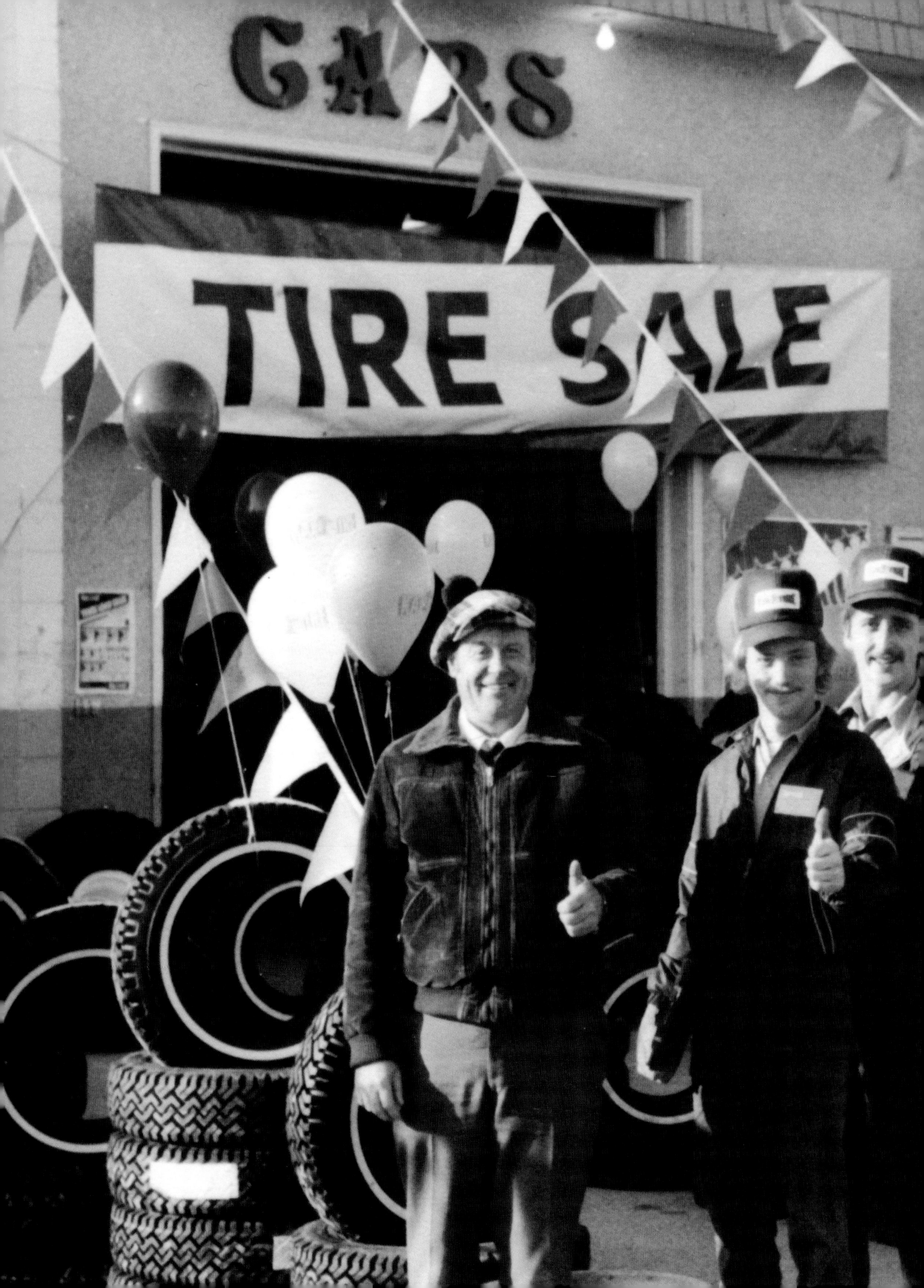
CARS
TIRE SALE

Archie tried to talk Tom out of it. "Coming from the perspective of a person born in 1942, I'd never seen hard times," he says. "I argued with him for 45 minutes. I told Tom we didn't have any fat to trim from this company. We were pretty lean. But he wouldn't leave it alone. He kept saying, 'Look again.'"

An obvious way to cut costs in a business slowdown is to lay off staff. Payroll, after all, is typically a service-based company's biggest expense. Kal's culture, a reflection of Tom's own, made layoffs difficult. The company had always insisted that employees' interests trumped the pursuit of profits. Kal attributed its success to the loyalty and dedication that employees had showed in return. To lay off staff to preserve the integrity of a bottom line seemed to violate the trust between employees and Kal that Tom had always held sacrosanct.

"We were a family company, in the sense that our employees and partners feel like family," Tom says. "You don't throw the relatives over the side when things get rough. If we did, I'd have worried about the kind of company we would become. The real bottom line means everybody pulling through a mess together."

The management team was still doubtful that Kal was carrying excess fat that it could hack away. But it obliged Tom and took a more acute look at Kal's expenses, and the executives' skepticism faded as they found places to trim. They promptly slashed advertising. They cut the inventory in the Vernon warehouse to reduce financing charges. They mothballed specially configured service trucks that weren't being used but were unlikely to find a buyer. They sold 18 other vehicles to escape costs such as depreciation, licensing, fuel and insurance. "We practically gave equipment away just to avoid the cost that went with it," says Tom.

Ironically, Tom himself wasn't quite so successful. Collecting receivables, his bailiwick, was just as critical to survival as cost controls. But characteristically, Tom couldn't bring himself to lean too heavily on customers suffering recessionary straits similar to Kal's. "One customer owed us $32,000 and was about to go bankrupt," Tom says. "I told him I had trust in him, and that he should place some trust in me. We worked out a commitment he could live with, and in two years he paid off the $32,000. Today the company's very successful and he's one of our biggest customers. He's thanked me so many times I can't count them all."

Inevitably, when Kal ran out of ways to cut costs, Tom was forced to agree to layoffs. Warehouses and retread plants were forced to lay off 15 percent of their employees. Stores had to do the same. For most managers at Kal, it was the worst thing they'd ever had to do, and they tried to handle the job as deftly as possible. Archie reminded the managers tasked with delivering bad news that employees deserved to be dealt with face-to-face whenever possible.

Archie, who considered laying people off the toughest job he'd had at Kal, handled the chore personally as often as he could. He met with small groups, lest there be misunderstandings about the Hobson's choice Kal was facing. "I told them, we can keep eight people and go broke, or keep six and continue to run the business," he says. "I promised that when we were successful again we'd hire them back, but in the meantime two of them had to find a job somewhere else."

HOTEL KAL

Kal Tire had never been in a financial position to offer lavish expense accounts. When looking for ways to lower costs, however, even the most modest allowances, no matter how legitimate, came under scrutiny. This practice turned Kal into the operator of a hostel patronized by tire guys.

One of the assets Kal inherited in the Advanx takeover was the warehouse under the Port Mann Bridge just outside Vancouver. At the time, it was common for Kal's salespeople to stay in hotels when doing business in Vancouver. Hoping to trim lodging costs, Kal converted part of the warehouse into a dorm for travelling staff, complete with kitchen facilities for preparing meals and morning coffee.

It would have been a stretch to call the dormitory idea popular. Overnighting tire men had to suffer noise from traffic and the occasional train overhead. As much as the hostel idea was a cost-saving measure, it hadn't escaped management's notice that it was also a reminder that frugality was the new watchword at Kal.

Getting that message across had a positive, albeit unintended, benefit. On any given night, the temporary residents occupying the partitioned units included both long-time Kal staff and those inherited from Advanx, a company that had been Kal's competitor. Sharing a pizza and a beer from the Kal-stocked fridge in the evening tended to wash away hard feelings from the past.

"After a takeover, feelings run high," says Don Knox, then Kal's head of inventory control. "But when you have to sleep in the same room as a guy you don't get on with, you'd better get over your differences. We could discuss a problem and come up with the best solution that night, because we had nothing else to do. We got a lot of work done."

LEARNING A TOUGH LESSON

By late 1982, as the country showed signs of shedding the weight of recession, Kal began making good on its promise to those it had laid off. The high proportion of returning employees confirmed the value of treating laid-off workers with as much dignity as possible. Not only was Kal able to realize its investment in their training, but it was also able to use it to get up to speed faster than if it had to bring in new people. In short, the principle of mutual trust between employer and employee, an extension of Tom Foord's personal creed that has become a prime ingredient of Kal's culture, had been tested in a crisis and had come through with flying colours.

Kal's young managers also weathered the crisis. Archie Stroh is convinced that handling unfamiliar business conditions hardened them and better prepared them to meet the future. "Any dummy can manage growth, but our young team learned to manage in a down time," he says. "When everything is sliding and you can do it right, you learn how to manage your business properly. It was the best thing that could have happened to us."

Tom Foord echoes the view. "It's good to have an extreme experience once in a while to bring you down to earth and make you really understand what the business world is all about," he says. "The recession made us better business people."

Remarkably, the slimming effort had actually resulted in Kal making a profit of $625,000 in 1982, on sales of about $45 million. It wasn't the profitability Kal hoped to achieve, and usually did, but it was at least black ink, something that eluded many businesses at the time.

Another positive result of the crisis management process, Larry Wynn believes, was improved communication. As well, watching expenses more closely became a practice embedded in everyday life at Kal. "The cutbacks were a whole bunch of little things, a little bit of everything," Larry says. "But the results were so dramatic that people started coming up with money-saving ideas everywhere. They never stopped, and collectively they continued to make a difference."

Although Kal was eventually able to hire back most of the employees that it had furloughed, it remained uncomfortable about having let them go in the first place. Doing so had distressed people — and people were the component of the business that Kal had always valued as the backbone of its organization. But even that had a positive result. The layoffs and rehirings focused Kal on employee retirement benefits — or lack thereof. And Ken Finch vowed to do something about it.

Like many Canadians at the time, Ken worried about the health of the Canada Pension Plan. Even if it survived, he felt that, combined with Kal's modest retirement program, the result would be an inadequate source of retirement income for a Kal employee. In 1983, as a newly minted partner in Kal Tire and a member of the senior management team, Ken began investigating alternatives. As a starting point, he focused on ways that Kal could broaden the existing profit-sharing plan, which primarily benefited store managers and assistants, to provide all employees with a secure future.

That Ken was thinking in that direction was a measure of the confidence that had come from managing through the recession. He believes it matured Kal in an operating sense, and better equipped its management to deal with growth. "It's the downturns that really separate the men from the boys," Ken says. "We became much better operators and because of what we learned, we were able to keep expanding."

Bob Barth (upper right) and Frank Hunter (bottom left) with fellow employees, framed in a tire at the Chilliwack store in the early 1980s.

MANPOWER MANAGEMENT IN A RECESSION

Laying off staff is one of the toughest jobs a manager has to do. But a story Ken Finch relates to management trainees demonstrates the fate of any company that refuses to make difficult manpower decisions.

Prior to the Advanx Tire purchase in 1981, Kal had been shopping for independent dealers in the Vancouver area that might be interested in joining Kal. On one occasion the search took Tom Foord, Archie Stroh and Ken — still relatively new to Kal — to the store of an acquaintance of Tom and Archie. The man had spent his entire working life as a credit manager for a major tire manufacturer, then quit late in his career to become a tire dealer. The three executives thought he might be a candidate to join Kal.

When they got to his store, however, they found a shattered dream. He'd invested in a store and equipment, and done well at first. At one point, he told his visitors, he'd had enough business to support 10 employees. But the recession in 1981 had hobbled his operation, and five years after his start-up, the business was broke. "When Tom, Archie and I went to see him, the store was shut down and everybody was gone," says Ken Finch. "Here was this 60-year-old guy who had just gone out of business. He lived upstairs over the store and all he had left was a second-hand car."

At first, Tom, Archie and Ken were puzzled by the failure and its cause. "Even he didn't seem entirely sure what he'd done wrong," Ken says. "He was pretty philosophical and said he wasn't sure about starting over at 60. But as we talked to him, he claimed to be proud of having done one thing right: no matter what the season, he told us, he'd never laid anyone off."

The Kal managers, of course, saw instantly the fatal flaw in the man's business thinking. "All I could think was, 'Wow, here's a guy who never understood what his responsibility was to his employees,'" says Ken. "Adjusting the workforce to the business is a fact of life in any business, but he didn't seem to get that at all."

Kal does, he adds. It hires temporary help in late fall when the first snowfall triggers a rush to install winter tires. But when store traffic drops off from December to February, it lays the temps off, bringing them back in the spring depending on business volume.

Ken acknowledges that it doesn't feel good letting people go. "But I've always thought of that guy who missed seeing his real responsibility to his employees. If he'd adjusted his manpower in the slow season and hired them back when it was busy, his business would have had a much better chance of surviving — and the workers he had laid off would still have had a job to come back to.

"Instead, he tried to be kind to his people and wound up doing the worst thing possible, compromising the future of everybody. It was a lesson I never forgot."

Kal Tire has always found creative ways to bring the company message to the local community — through focused advertising, grand openings that became media events, and even small-town parades like this one.

KAL TIRE CATERS TO YOUR TIRE NEEDS

CHAPTER FIVE:
THE POST-RECESSION BOUNCE

(THE LATE 1980s)

MANAGING THE COMEBACK

Even before the recession began subsiding in late 1982, it had been apparent to Kal management that it couldn't ignore marketing if it hoped to recover along with the economy. After all, the public couldn't put off buying tires forever. Kal had 30 stores to promote, and tire deals to advertise if it hoped to position itself to take a share of the sales.

Placing a new emphasis on marketing was a relief to Richard Hamilton. He'd been hired in 1973 to handle transportation and warehousing. His ability to handle a wide range of jobs was a tribute to his versatility. But adding marketing and advertising to his other duties proved to be too much. To give Richard some relief, it was decided marketing and advertising functions would be split. And Archie Stroh figured he found the ideal person to take advertising off Richard's plate.

Tom Serviss, a 33-year-old former professional hockey player who turned to selling business machines, counted Kal among his customers. On sales calls Tom had frequently inquired about openings at Kal. Archie finally offered him a job in 1982. After the customary initiation changing tires in a Vernon store, Archie figured the extroverted Tom was worth trying out as advertising manager, under Richard Hamilton.

Tom Serviss had some reservations. Not least of them was the fact that he knew next to nothing about creating ads. Archie, however, dismissed his concern, pointing out that common sense, accountability and personality were the main requirements to do the job. "And you've got all three," he told Tom.

Despite his lack of background, Tom Serviss waded in. Seventy percent of Kal's business at the time was commercial, and only 30 percent retail. To grow the retail end, Tom began modestly with newspaper ads that offered special deals. But he recognized that retail customers felt intimidated by the truckers, miners and forestry workers they met at Kal's stores, who accounted for the bulk of Kal's business. "People would read Kal's ads and come to Kal Tire to buy, and a kid would come out from under the back of a logging truck wiping grease from his hands."

Tom Serviss began putting his somewhat undersized $300,000 budget to work. To make stores more retail-friendly and less industrial, he introduced a new Kal policy that employees wear gloves and place protective covers on steering wheels and seats of cars in for service. He ran Truckload Tire Sales, towing trailer-loads of tires into town and selling them at sale prices. To create some excitement around its decidedly mundane products, he promoted the events with parades, balloons and streamers, free hotdogs and popcorn. "It turned out to be a pretty good promotion for the money," says Archie Stroh.

TELL THEM
TOM SENT YOU

Swapping his promotions hat for his advertising one, Tom Serviss stole a page from Chrysler. The automaker's president, Lee Iacocca, had become a television star and helped turn his company around by appearing confident and trustworthy in television commercials. Tom Serviss figured Kal could use a similarly credible spokesperson, whose character consumers would associate with honesty and decency — and with Kal — when making tire-buying decisions.

Kal didn't have to look much farther than down the hall to Tom Foord's office for an appropriate spokesperson. "Tom was the key," says Tom Serviss. "He was our best salesman, he talked well, and we sure didn't need any market research to prove that."

In the commercials, Tom Foord delivered the tag line, "And tell them Tom Foord sent you." Tom Serviss knew he had a hit on his hands almost as soon as the ads appeared. Stores began reporting customers repeating the line when they came in. A boost in employee pride was an unexpected result: employees, whether in the stores or the Vernon office, noticeably puffed up with pride as Tom Foord became a provincial icon by championing their company on television.

Tom Serviss had cleverly leveraged Tom Foord's unexpected celebrity to stretch Kal's ad budget. At new-stores openings Tom Foord, senior management and the local mayor all took part in the ribbon-cutting. Tom Foord was especially a draw in small towns. "All of a sudden everybody wanted to meet the guy they'd seen on TV who was in their town," says Tom Serviss.

Kal even successfully took on the giant Canadian Tire chain when it expanded into Western Canada. Despite its name, Canadian Tire mostly sells a range of housewares, sporting goods and hardware. Kal emphasized its focus solely on tires with ads that featured a hockey goalie ridiculously plastered with duck decoys, toilet seats and toasters. Tom Foord, standing at centre ice in a Kal Tire jacket, then pointed out to viewers that, "We don't sell toasters and hockey sticks, we only sell tires. Tell them Tom Foord sent you!" As a kicker, Tom Serviss skated in and scored on the Canadian Tire goalie.

Although the recession left many independent tire dealers staggering, it wasn't Kal's style to gloat over its own survival. "We felt for a lot of those folks," says Archie Stroh. "Sure they were competitors, but we knew what many of them had gone through and sympathized."

Even so, having steered itself carefully around most of the recessionary potholes, Kal recognized opportunity in the troubles of its competitors. In some cases, financially strapped tire dealers were eager to cut their losses and get out of the tire business. Increasingly, Kal emerged as their buyer of choice. Kal didn't beat up sellers on price, and treated acquired companies' employees, suppliers and customers with respect.

Opposite: A still of Tom taken from a TV commercial for Kal's customer protection policy, in the early 1990s — in the mid-1980s, Tom's ease in front of the camera made him the obvious choice as Kal Tire's spokesman. **Above:** Shooting a TV commercial in the late 1980s — Tom always closed with the line, "And tell them Tom Foord sent you."

As it became part of its competitors' exit strategy, Kal embarked on another modest growth spurt. In 1984, the company purchased Vancouver-based D&D Tires for about $11 million from owner Gary Dickinson, adding five new outlets to Kal's growing chain and strengthening its presence in the West's biggest urban market.

Elsewhere, however, geography continued to be a challenge. Distribution to stores hundreds of miles apart was costly. To improve economies, Tom and Archie were always looking for opportunities for additional locations.

But by far the best business opportunity Kal had in years turned out to be the B.C. government's decision to build the Coquihalla highway, a project similar to the Rogers Pass section of the Trans Canada that had helped Kal establish its credentials.

THE ATTRACTIONS OF COAL

For the most part, Kal's mining team, put together in the mid-1970s and 1980s, had done a reasonable job serving copper, gold and silver mines. Growth of sales had been modest — steady rather than spectacular. But as time progressed Joe Peshko, Flemming Sorensen and later George Frame often found themselves playing catch-up when they made sales pitches to the growing number of coal mines coming on stream in the province.

Flemming, whom Archie had hired away from a Firestone dealer in 1981, had had little luck in the coal fields around Sparwood in the Kootenays southeast of Vernon. He'd found that Crown Tire of Edmonton had locked up contracts to sell Bridgestone tires to most of the mines in the area. And he struck out trying to sell Goodyear OTR tires.

He had better luck in 1982 when he turned his attentions to a new coal mine opening in Tumbler Ridge, a five-hour drive northeast of Prince George. The mine had contracts to supply Japanese buyers and was expected to become Canada's biggest open-pit operation. And for a change, Kal was on the scene early. Flemming's repeated calls on operators of the mine finally resulted in Kal winning a contract with Quintette Coal.

Tom and Archie had their eyes on Lyle Kennedy to manage its Tumbler Ridge operation. He'd been a Kal Tire customer since Jim Lochhead had replaced his tires that floated away in a flood back in 1972. A veteran equipment manager with experience at mines, power dams and construction sites, Lyle was an expert in section repairs (reconstructing tire sidewalls), and was renowned as a mechanical innovator used to problem solving on the job.

Lyle also turned out to be a shrewd negotiator. Though generally a valued trait at Kal, it created a minor hitch to his hiring. He agreed to take the job, but only on the condition that he could start after goose-hunting season. Tom Foord, himself a passionate goose hunter, fully understood where Lyle was coming from and agreed to wait three weeks.

TAKING ON THE COQUIHALLA HIGHWAY

The Kamloops store under Colin Campbell had been successful. But Kal Tire felt a second outlet, focusing solely on commercial tires and OTRs, was warranted. Initially, the idea had been to serve local mining activity around Kamloops. But the provincial government's announcement that it was going ahead with construction of the Coquihalla Highway was good news at Kal.

The provincial government intended the proposed road, a multi-lane freeway, to begin in Hope on the Trans-Canada Highway in the south and terminate in Kamloops in the north. There was a push to complete the 195-kilometre section, which would go through inhospitable geography that included an avalanche-protection shed in the Cascade Mountains, to facilitate passage to Vancouver from Alberta and the interior of B.C. in time for Expo 86.

To Tom, the opportunity for Kal was a replay of the Rogers Pass highway project that had boosted Kal's fortunes in the late 1950s and into the early 1960s. Robert Kehler, who was then looking after the new OTR store in Kamloops, oversaw the necessary workforce, equipment and tires to service the various road-building vehicles expected to be involved in the Coquihalla project.

Though still inexperienced in projects of Coquihalla's scale — Rogers Pass had been 20 years earlier — Kal's technical teams had expertise in tire handling, a foundation they could quickly build on. "We learned how to change every size of tire there was, and we did it at all hours of the night," says Robert. "Then we learned how to source tires, because everybody was clamouring for them. Once we got the hang of it, we learned how to solicit even more business. We never stopped working, and the store was a huge success."

In the end, the Coquihalla only barely met the deadline — some sections weren't completed until 1987 — and its total cost of $848 million vastly outran the projected initial $550-million budget. But the mega project was a profitable success from Kal's perspective: it became yet another demonstration of its tire-handling and supply capabilities in the field, helping burnish its reputation in markets requiring OTR expertise.

"Lyle soon proved an ability to make sacrifices and perform under pressure in tough circumstances — characteristics that had established Kal's reputation for service in the field."

Lyle soon proved an ability to make sacrifices and perform under pressure in tough circumstances, characteristics that had established Kal's reputation for service in the field. When Lyle arrived, Tumbler Ridge wasn't much more sophisticated than the blind he'd recently occupied to hunt geese, so he bought a camper to live in. But there was little room on the crowded mine site for subcontractors so Lyle became a nomad, setting up camp wherever he could around town. When Quintette got around to making lots available to miners and contractors, Lyle bought enough to house Kal Tire's 13 men working on site. Within the year, Lyle's wife, Valerie, and their children moved up to join him.

The Kennedy family exemplified the civic spirit and participation in community life that was typical of the sort of citizens Kal tended to attract. To celebrate B.C. declaring Tumbler Ridge a town, Valerie baked a giant six-foot-by-four-foot cake decorated with mountains, the town hall, mining trucks and trains loaded with coal.

Not surprisingly, having so enthusiastically embraced life in the town, the Kennedys were sorry to leave four years later in 1986 when they moved to Vernon where Kal felt Lyle would be able to apply his inventiveness and engineering skills more broadly as head of technical services at Kal.

In his new capacity, Lyle demonstrated that Kal was more about service than merely a supplier of tires or crews of bead-breakers. His talent, in fact, indirectly continued to benefit Tumbler Ridge long after he left the town, as well as in mining camps all over B.C.

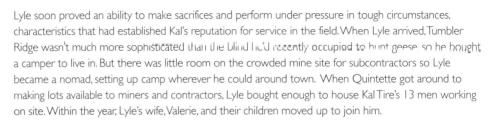

WEIGHING IN
WITH TECHNOLOGY

Lyle Kennedy had a rare talent for exploiting technology to develop systems that solve tire problems he'd recognized in the field. He knew, for instance, that miners routinely overloaded mining trucks, one of the most common abuses of tires. So at the Quintette Coals site in Tumbler Ridge he installed scales.

Unfortunately, the truck-and-load weighing system he borrowed from Goodyear turned out to be poorly engineered for the job. Goodyear's apparent disinterest in operating the scales wasn't a ringing endorsement for their use, either; the tire maker would truck them to a mine site, but then leave them there with little follow-up.

Goodyear's attitude was perhaps understandable. A failure that required a user to buy a new tire wasn't, after all, a disaster as far as the tire manufacturer was concerned. Poorly designed equipment bothered Lyle's engineering sensibility, though. "The scales were built with the wrong kind of load-scale and the wrong kind of electronics, and they failed constantly," he says. "They were hydraulic, so in cold weather the equipment froze up. More often than not they'd be broken when we arrived to use them."

Convinced of the merit in weighing trucks in order to prevent premature tire destruction due to overloading and uneven load distribution, Lyle designed a scale system that used new technology. Kal then commissioned Pacific Scales in Vancouver to manufacture a scale of Lyle's design, which featured four electronic load-cells and special pads onto which the trucks drove. The scales were robust enough to handle equipment of up to two million pounds per axle, yet precise enough to weigh vehicles within a 1.5 percent accuracy range. Once it weighed a truck, the system generated a load-profile report noting tonnage and evenness of loading, both crucial to tire maintenance, longevity and safety.

Lyle's system soon became the industry standard, recognized as the best set of mining-truck scales available. The entire unit, which weighs only 10,000 pounds, is portable, helping make it an effective traveling advertisement for Kal's technological prowess. Kal's transport division has hauled the scales, including its heated scale-room and an office, all over North America. "I flew to the mining sites to operate them." says Lyle "They were in demand constantly, and booked months in advance."

Lyle also participated in the development of Tire Track, Kal's software system designed to monitor such things as wear, usage patterns and maintenance/replacement schedules in order to improve safety and productivity of off-road, commercial and fleet operators. Tire Track has since been refined to take advantage of newer technology.

Systems like mine-site scales and Tire Track technology are part of Kal's constantly improving service offerings. They're also a tribute to employees like Lyle Kennedy, whose inventiveness resulted in a better way to do a job. These industry advancements are representative of a half-century tradition at Kal of helping customers improve their efficiency.

I flew to the mining sites to operate them. They were in demand constantly, and booked months in advance.

KAL GOES PUBLIC...ALMOST

All businesses with growth ambitions face the challenge of finding sufficient capital at an affordable price. Those that elect to borrow to finance growth must generate a big enough return on borrowed capital to show a profit after servicing the debt.

Kal, however, tried to avoid debt as a means of funding growth. It preferred to reinvest the bulk of its profits in the business. Instead of taking money out of the company in the form of profit sharing, bonuses or dividends, Kal's shareholders — its partners who were also senior managers — normally left the money in an account that the company can use to expand.

The practice kept the cost of capital low and facilitated growth. But it didn't do much for its shareholders' bank accounts, at least in the short term. Tom Foord, for instance, was 63 years old in the mid-1980s. And most of the money he'd made in 35 years in business was tied up in Kal. Tom still had ambitions to expand Kal, however, and he and George Miller began exploring alternative means of financing the expansion while also unlocking some of his wealth.

One obvious answer was to do an initial public offering (IPO) of shares in Kal. For virtually all of his adult life, Tom had been under financial strain and beholden to the banks. By "going public," he'd sell shares to investors to raise capital. Since he was Kal's biggest shareholder, he could cash in some of his stock and take a breather.

An IPO would also enable Kal to reward employees and long-time executives who had helped build the company, with stock ownership. Since the market value would rise and fall in concert with Kal's corporate performance, employees theoretically would have an incentive to perform well: they would push up the share price and in the process increase their own wealth as well as that of outside shareholders.

Of course, if Kal didn't perform, the value of its shares — and the wealth of shareholders — would decline. But companies contemplating going public seldom think negatively. And Tom admits that he and George Miller didn't either, at first. Rather, they were seduced somewhat by the positives of doing an IPO. "We were going to get a big chunk of money and all my financial worries would be over," says Tom.

The further along they got in the process, however, the more caveats arose. Preparing a prospectus raised one flag. A prospectus is a public document that, under securities law, must provide explicit insight into the financial and operational details of the business. It is intended to be scrutinized by prospective investors.

When Tom and George saw the prospectus for Kal, they saw one hidden cost in going public. In addition to detailing financial information, a prospectus must include arrangements with suppliers and customers — precisely the sort of thing they'd spent their entire business lives guarding. Now not only investors but also competitors would have access to the intimate details of Kal's business.

The more Tom and George thought about the implications of the prospectus, the more expensive the capital they'd be raising through the IPO began to look: they'd raise plenty of money, but the cost was high — Kal's independence. "When you go public in the tire business, all your secrets are open to the customer and the supplier," Tom says. "As a private company you can choose who you give this information to, and who you don't. This independence was important to me."

In fact, it occurred to Tom that going public might actually put a damper on growth, the opposite of what he and George had hoped to achieve through the IPO. "We wouldn't be able to grow without having to get everybody's approval," he says.

Opposite:
Vancouver independent tire dealer Dale Parson started out a doubter when he heard about Kal Tire's reputation for fairness in its acquisitions, but became a true believer when he retired and sold his operation to Kal.

KAL'S SECRET WEAPON:
DEAL HONOURABLY

Kal's acquisition style — an open and fair process that showed respect for the seller — was an extension of the way it routinely conducted business. But it was different enough from the norm in the tire business that many were dubious when told of Kal's generosity toward owners of businesses it bought.

Dale Parson, an independent Vancouver tire dealer, was one of the doubters. He had been a friend of Archie Stroh's since the 1960s. After Kal started its associate program, Archie and Tom repeatedly tried to sign Dale up, but the industry veteran preferred his independence and resisted their entreaties.

Dale remained friendly with Archie, however, and when Kal paid Gary Dickinson a reported $11 million in 1984 for the five-store D & D Tire chain in Vancouver, Dale offered to help Archie take inventory of the assets. But while he thought much of what he was trying to price was worthless, Archie insisted on counting it all as new inventory and paying Gary on that basis.

"I was curious about what was going on," Dale says. "But when I asked Tom about it later, he told me it was part of Kal's policy. He said, 'If you pay a little more for a business, the added value you'll get from that overpayment will more than compensate for the money.' Tom figured the owner getting the good price would have nothing but good to say about Kal and that that would benefit Kal down the road."

Dale admits he still wasn't sure about the strategy six years later when he decided to retire and Kal agreed to buy his business. But as the deal was put together, he became a believer. "When they treated me with the same generosity I'd seen with D & D Tire, I thought it was because we were friends," says Dale. "They weren't aggressive, and if it wasn't a good deal for both sides it wasn't a deal. It was just how they do business."

Dale's story might have ended there, with Kal paying him well for his business. But in 2002, when Archie offered him a job as head of associate dealer development in B.C., he accepted right away. "By then I'd seen enough to recognize that everything I'd heard about Kal was true," he says. "The company really was something special."

Over the next seven years, Dale reaffirmed his view by making sure that new associates were treated fairly and generously, as was Kal's custom. "I have never seen a single dealer walk away unhappy from a transaction with Kal," he says. "After every purchase, even dealers who didn't stay with Kal remained friends and kept in touch."

Fair dealing, Dale says, wasn't the only differentiator he spotted between Kal and its competitors as he traveled the province scouting potential associates. He cites safety as another distinction. "At Kal eye-and-ear protection is just taken for granted," he says. "You won't see the T-Lock (invented by Ken Finch) in any other shops, or portable cages on their service trucks either. When our guys work on a truck tire, it's locked down and caged, so there's no chance of them being hurt."

Dale, now in his 60s, has no plans to re-retire. "I'm like most at Kal," he says. "I think of it as being partly mine and I can hardly wait to get up in the morning to get to work. It's one of the things about Kal Tire that I haven't noticed anywhere else: nobody seems to want to retire, or stay retired. We're still having too much fun."

Even the prospect of heading out on the customary dog-and-pony show to drum up interest from potential stockholders seemed un-Kal-like. They'd be trumpeting Kal's virtues to investment dealers who would be selling its stock to the public, a major departure for a company whose values had always reflected the unassuming nature of its founder.

After six months of discussion, Tom and George decided that Kal Tire should remain private. They aborted the IPO. "In the end I decided that finances should not be the main reason to be pushed into being a public company," Tom says.

> *By then I'd seen enough to recognize that everything I'd heard about Kal was true. The company really was something special.*

COLUMBIA TIRE...
AND A REUNION
WITH MICHELIN

Throughout the first half the 1980s, Kal's attempt to sign contracts with mining companies was often thwarted by the presence of Columbia Tire's salespeople already on the site. That Kal had won business in spite of the disadvantage, and that it had operated in an above-board manner, hadn't escaped notice of Columbia's owner, Verne Bullock.

In 1985, when Verne was looking to exit the mining-tire business in Alberta and the interior of B.C., he offered to sell Kal his Edmonton outlet that did most of the OTR sales in Alberta. Kal had jumped at the chance to expand its OTR market and at the same time eliminate a competitor. Verne had been so impressed at how smoothly the 1985 sale in Alberta had gone, that he approached Kal again in 1987 when he was seeking a buyer for Columbia Tire's B.C. operations.

The acquisition, which would cost about $24 million, trumped the Advanx takeover to become Kal's biggest yet. Coupled with the Advanx purchase, the new acquisition built on Kal's move from the interior to B.C.'s Lower Mainland. Columbia's assets included seven stores in the Vancouver area, and a warehouse and retread plant on Annacis Island in the Fraser River in Delta, B.C.

Not wishing to alert the industry to the transaction prior to its completion, representatives of the two companies met off-site in a Vancouver hotel. Tom, George Miller and Kal's lawyer were at the meeting. Archie, who was most familiar with the business assets and people involved, handled most of the negotiations. His ebullient style had such an impact on Columbia's lawyer that at the conclusion of the meeting he promised, "I'll get this tidied up and give it to your lawyer, Mr. Stroh." As well as integrating the Columbia stores, Kal would be absorbing more than 100 new employees. Doug Starling, whose father

worked for Columbia at the time, recalls the angst among Columbia employees who suddenly found themselves employed by a new owner. "There's often a lot of distress after an acquisition," says Doug, who himself later joined Kal. "A lot of misinformation goes on in the background, and you have all these nervous people who don't know if they're going to like the new company, or the rules and regulations. Quite often they don't."

Kris Stromdahl, who had been on the order desk at Columbia Tire at the time of Kal's takeover, embodied the concern at Columbia. He was getting fed up with flux in the tire business and was considering leaving it altogether rather than staying on under Kal. "I kept waiting for the other shoe to drop," he says. "I worked for Firestone and they closed all their stores across Canada. I worked for Columbia and they sold out to Kal Tire. I thought maybe it's time for me to go back to school and do something else."

While he was making up his mind, Kris happened to overhear Tom, Archie, Ken Finch and Bruce Cantalope discussing some business. "Once I heard them and watched them in action, I knew I wanted to be here," he says. Other key Columbia people were also impressed with Kal. Doug Starling's father Derry stayed on, as did Jerry Wong, a future head of Kal's industrial division. Kris Stromdahl went on to become a senior zone manager at Kal.

A windfall in the Columbia purchase was the reunification of Kal and French tire-maker Michelin. The two had fallen out over a retreading process called Renovex that Michelin had developed for replacing the belts on a radial tire. Kal became a Renovex franchisee, which required it to import radial-tire belts from Michelin in France. But by 1982 the price of the belts had risen to the point that Kal was losing money on Renovex retreading.

When Michelin proved deaf to its complaints and refused to adjust its pricing, Kal dropped its Renovex franchise. The battle escalated when Michelin countered by summarily cutting Kal as a dealer of its tires. Archie had to placate Kal Tire's salesmen who were upset at losing a good-selling product. His strategy was to remind them that Kal was becoming more than a purveyor of tires. "I pointed out that in this business we sell ourselves and our services," he says.

Kal hadn't been pleased with what it considered high-handed action by Michelin, but decided to move on without having the company's products to sell. When Tom learned, six years later during conversations with a lawyer on another matter, that Kal had a good case for sueing Michelin, he decided to go ahead with the action.

As it happened, the suit was still before the courts in 1987. And it became more complicated when Kal began negotiating the Columbia Tire takeover. When Michelin had broken its relationship with Kal over Renovex, Columbia had assumed the role of Michelin's biggest dealer in B.C. Now that Kal was buying Columbia, Michelin had to decide either to make peace with Kal, clearly a growing force in the B.C. tire business, or establish a relationship with another dealer.

One thing was sure about the impasse: Tom Foord had no intention of approaching Michelin. It had been his policy for his entire career never to make the first conciliatory move in a dispute with a supplier. Besides, Kal's suit against Michelin was still outstanding. In the event, Tom won the waiting game when Jean Pochet, newly installed as Michelin Canada's president, contacted Tom — who was in a goose-hunting blind at the time — to seek a resolution.

Tom's natural affinity for fence mending took over when he subsequently met with Jean Pochet. The two tire men represented the two sides of the business that were often at loggerheads. But to their surprise, they found they actually liked each other. They quickly agreed that it made sense for both Kal and Michelin that the tire-maker resume its relationship with Kal as a supplier.

It wasn't Kal's style then — or ever, for that matter — to crow in victory. But Archie acknowledges a sense of gratification among Kal managers at the news. "Michelin had put all its eggs into the Columbia Tire basket," he says. "We had the pleasure of seeing it having to admit its mistake." He was also pleased to be able to tell Kal's salespeople that they could once again include Michelin's popular radial tires in their product line.

But the most satisfying aspect of the incident was that Kal had reached a size that it had been able to use as leverage with a supplier. To Tom, who battled with suppliers for more than 35 years, the Michelin agreement was yet another validation of Kal's growth strategy.

ALBERTA BOUND

It had always been Kal's practice to give individual managers a reasonable degree of autonomy in running their stores with a minimum of head-office control. To be sure, there were guidelines they had to follow. But the theory was that store managers, who lived in the community, best understood their individual local markets and knew best how to serve them.

The operating style had worked for the most part. But acquisitions in the mid-1980s had expanded the number of stores. Oversight by the smallish management group in Vernon became increasingly difficult to maintain. The fact was, standards occasionally slipped. Bruce Cantalope, vice-president of stores, saw as one of his challenges a need to tighten controls enough to stem the slide, but without dulling nimbleness and entrepreneurial spirit of the individual managers.

In 1984, Bruce had begun developing systems to introduce greater consistency and accountability to store operations. But when he'd run into a trouble spot, he had been able to call on Kal's resident trouble-shooter, Robert Kehler, to manoeuvre around it.

Robert's success had cast him as a rising star at Kal. After his tours of duty as a fixer in Merritt and Lumby, Robert was promoted to zone manager. And when Bruce called on the nine-year veteran at Kal to do some triage on the money-losing Edmonton store, Robert yet again delivered above and beyond the objective to add order to Kal's Alberta operations. The 32-year-old hit Alberta like a prairie duster. On the way to Edmonton in the company plane, Robert dropped in on an acquaintance who was managing an independent tire outlet in Grande Prairie, west of Edmonton. When Robert left town, he'd vetted the operation as a good candidate as a Kal outlet. Within weeks Kal bought it.

In Edmonton, Robert determined the reason the Yellowhead Trail store was underperforming; he promptly fired the manager for theft. Turning his energy to the store's poor sales, he refocused its activities on its local market. "It had a terrible business model," he says. "It had been trying to bring in customers from as far away as Calgary and all the way up to the Northwest Territories."

Robert hired Ed Lauer as assistant manager in Edmonton, then moved on to address the absence of a Kal outlet in Calgary. His first effort faltered. The Calgary dealer he signed up as a Kal associate, though eager to reap the benefits of a Kal relationship, was less so when it came to accepting the responsibility that came with being part of the Kal family. "We believed in long hours, hard work and service," says Robert. "But they believed in getting what you could get and closing the store at five o'clock." Never one to dwell on setbacks, Robert cut his losses. "Eventually we got a divorce, and separated their business and ours, right down to the receivables and the service trucks."

Robert's extensive industry Rolodex, and the respect of those in it, allies and competitors alike, frequently benefited Kal. Danny Funk, for instance, was an old friend; Robert knew he'd be perfect to fill the managerial void in the Grande Prairie outlet that Kal set up as a corporate-owned store. Danny, who had been operating an independent tire store with a friend in Grimshaw, Alberta, two hours north of Grande Prairie, admits he was wary about the tire business. He hadn't been getting rich in Grimshaw. Robert's sales pitch outlined Kal's potential, corporate resources and, not incidentally, its profit-sharing plan. "I knew there was no way Kal could be growing so fast and not be true to its word," Danny says, "so I decided to give it a try."

Danny's hiring proved that Robert's misstep in selecting a Calgary manager had been the exception rather than the rule. By 1990, Danny was such a success in Grande Prairie that he too was promoted to zone manager.

ENTER THE ZONE MANAGERS

When Ken Finch joined Kal in 1980, he'd gone through the customary Kal initiation process, which involved working on the shop floor and in various positions in a company store. "It hardly made me an expert in tires," he says, "but it helped me appreciate how important Kal's team members are in offering service."

There was ample evidence that Kal had done a lot of things right. But as an engineer, Ken was predisposed to more systematic organizational models than Kal had developed to that point. He felt that a more clearly defined structure would facilitate even better management throughout the company. The question was, what should the appropriate structure look like?

In evaluating models, Ken and Bruce Cantalope were leery of losing concepts that had worked at Kal. Personal contact between senior management in head office and store managers, for instance, had been central to Kal's success. Ken didn't want to lose that. Yet he could see that as the company grew and units became more dispersed, one-on-one relationships would be harder to establish and maintain.

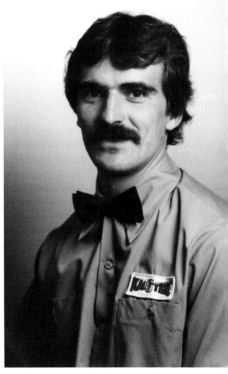

Opposite, from top: Verne Bullock, Columbia Tire owner who sold to Kal Tire. Derry Starling, an employee of Columbia, was impressed with Kal Tire's approach to business and stayed on after the sale. His son Doug Starling was already working for Kal Tire when it bought Columbia Tire. Jerry Wong became head of Kal Tire's industrial division. **Above:** Robert Kehler became a rising star in the company after turning money-losing stores around.

They rejected the idea of itinerant supervisors who dropped into stores to assist managers with problems — and to make suggestions on their operations. Bruce and Ken felt that without experiencing the same day-to-day issues that store managers faced, supervisors would lack credibility. They also didn't think supervisors would — or should — try to gain the confidence of store managers based solely on the authority vested in them by head office. Ken had experienced first-hand the discomfort of managing people who knew more than he did. "Not long after I came to the company, I was handing out advice to managers when they knew full well I'd never run a store," says Ken. "It was a very weak kind of supervision."

At Tom Foord's suggestion, Ken and Bruce looked at a concept employed by Les Schwab, a long-time mentor and friend of Tom's. Les employed a "zone manager" model in his tire business, one of the biggest and most successful independent dealership chains in the U.S. Kal's management concluded that the Schwab system would also work as their organizing structure.

The principle behind the system is that supervising by showing is better than telling. Instead of working out of a central office, zone managers would operate their own outlets as exemplars of efficiency. The so-called model store got everything right, from customer service and staff training, to accounts receivable and inventory.

As well as managing his own store, a zone manager would be responsible for overseeing managers of four or five other outlets in his area. If he needed to show any of them an ideal way to handle a store system or concept, he could use his own model store to demonstrate both the system and the standard they were expected to follow at their outlets.

The beauty of the system from the zone managers' perspective, says Ken Finch, is that the managers under their supervision tend to listen. "When you run a model store yourself, you have the credibility to supervise," says Ken. "It's a tremendously powerful way of managing."

Another attraction of the zone manager system is its capacity to train managers as decision-makers. Ken felt in-house training was necessary to make up for the general lack of higher education at Kal. "There were no university graduates among Kal's store managers," he says. "Most had typically dropped out of high school and taken a job with Kal and become tire guys whom Kal tried to turn into salesmen and managers."

That Kal had done so successfully was a credit to the managers' own contribution, intelligence and energy. "They could think on their feet much better than I could, and they dealt with customers better than I did," he says. "But most of them never had the opportunity to learn the discipline it takes to make decisions on an ongoing basis."

The zone manager system helped fill that void in training. And by training a proven commodity — the store's own personnel — rather than going to the expense of recruiting outside the company and starting from scratch, its training programs become more productive. Essentially, Kal would be putting its faith and resources into those who'd already showed their capability and loyalty.

The zone manager system had a number of other key attributes. It gives team members a clear path to self-improvement so it becomes an incentive that benefits both employees and Kal. It also enables the company to grow while maintaining a flat management structure. Instead of a layer of middle managers, Kal has zone managers who also run a store.

The concept has helped Kal maintain cultural continuity, too. Annual store visits by senior management had been a long-held tradition at Kal in order to put a face on senior management for store managers. But the visits have proved difficult to maintain as Kal has grown. While the company has no intention of eliminating the annual store visits, zone managers — typically veteran store operators with ties to head office — fill in the gaps.

When you run a model store yourself, you have the credibility to supervise. It's a tremendously powerful way of managing.

Opposite: Norm Schmidt, the senior zone manager for the retread division at the Chilliwack plant he manages, holding a photo of the original Abbotsford plant team.

For all its benefits, growth had the potential to render the structure cumbersome; as Kal grew, the number of zone managers also increased. Kal found an answer for that eventuality, too. It created senior zone managers who had oversight for a group of zone managers. Senior zone managers — like zone managers — also ran a model store, so they too had credibility when mentoring zone and store managers. "Without that structure we'd probably have hired a new level of middle-management to go out and tell store managers what to do," Ken Finch says. "The whole nature of our expansion would have turned out very differently."

MAKING ZONE MANAGEMENT WORK

When Kal went about putting its new structure in place, appointing Robert Kehler a zone manager was a slam-dunk. Other zone managers in the early stages of the program arrived at Kal via different routes, but had similarly distinguished themselves. Kris Stromdahl, the former Columbia Tire employee who stayed on with Kal after being impressed by its management, had gone on to become Kal's first marketing manager of retread operations, and then its first training coordinator.

As manager of the Coquitlam store and a new zone manager, Kris tried to sustain what he calls the connectedness between management and store staffs that he remembered resulting from visits to his store by Tom, Archie or Bruce Cantalope. "Maybe it was because they all came from small towns that made them so well grounded," says Kris, now a senior zone manager working out of the Port Kells location. "The secret of the organization today is that it's still driven by the qualities of the original partners. They set the tone with their ethics and values."

Far from stifling creativity through the use of formulas and rigid procedures as franchisors often do, Kal's structure actually seemed to stimulate it. In his Grande Prairie store, for example, Danny Funk had encouraged employees to call themselves consultants rather than salespeople when dealing with commercial customers. He felt it helped them stay focused on customer service, a Kal staple.

The beauty of the zone management as far as Danny is concerned is that it enables good ideas to gain currency quickly and get passed from store to store. Good ideas also have a higher acceptance rate when explained and endorsed by zone managers and senior zone managers than when distributed via memo from Vernon.

"We had some pretty stiff competition out there," says Danny, who later graduated to zone manager and senior zone manager. "We started providing services like tire tracking, so we could give our customers in forestry and the oil patch business the lowest cost per mile. As a consultant, you gain customer loyalty. Your customer realizes you are working in his best interests by trying to lower his costs. That's the biggest reason we grew the way we did. We really worked on building loyalty."

Ed Lauer, trained by Robert Kehler as an assistant manager in Edmonton, made it a practice after being appointed zone manager to treat store managers under his supervision as he'd been treated. According to Ed, a strength of the zone system was that it didn't feature guys in suits who arrived on the manager's doorstep to deliver edicts and instructions from head office.

More to the point, Ed's approach perpetuates the Kal culture throughout the organization, much as a parent might instill family values in its child through example. "The managers know we've been there and still manage a store," Ed says. "We earn their respect by showing respect in return for the challenges they're dealing with. We challenge each other until we arrive at the same vision, but the managers trust that what we're trying to do is in their best interest, to make their job easier and more effective, and not some hidden agenda."

The secret of the organization today is that it's still driven by the qualities of the original partners. They set the tone with their ethics and values.

KAL'S INTERNAL AUDITOR

Tom's policy for 35 years not to hire family hadn't been easy. For years, his father had been entreating him to hire his brother Ian who worked for an auto parts company. "But Ian and I were good friends," says Tom in explaining his reluctance. "I dreaded the thought of what would happen if things didn't work out. We got along too well for me to jeopardize our relationship."

After Tom hired Ken Finch in 1980, however, he softened somewhat on the issue. When Ian approached him in 1986, he was ready to bend his rule again. But to avoid any suggestion of nepotism, he left the decision on his brother's hiring to Archie, who knew Ian. Archie saw no reason not to put him on Kal's payroll and assigned him to the purchasing department with responsibility for buying vehicles and parts for Kal.

Ian soon earned his keep when he remarked that unexplained price discrepancies on purchases were going unnoticed and costing Kal money. On the purchasing side, in the beginning Ian was intimidated by the size of the deals he was negotiating. He'd come from a company where $1,000 was big money; at Kal the first asset he bought was a specially equipped truck that cost close to $200,000. "I called Bruce Cantalope and told him there was no bloody way I was going to spend that much money," Ian says. "Bruce told me, 'Just order it,' and I thought 'Oh my God, I just spent nearly a quarter of a million dollars.'"

Another of Ian's jobs was monitoring corporate credit cards, a special interest of George Miller's. "George Miller hated credit cards," Ian says. "Every time he came into the office he'd ask, 'Are you checking all the credit cards? Keep the rope tight on all of them.' I was even in charge of monitoring gas purchases, and pointing out to guys, who were buying two tanks of gas in one day, to stop filling their wife's car on company money."

In the end, Ian stayed at Kal for 11 years and vindicated Tom's decision to hire a family member, according to Archie. "He performed impeccably," he says. In a way, Ian may also have set the stage for his nephew Robert's arrival at Kal as well.

But that event didn't happen as fast or as smoothly as Tom had hoped.

Above: Tom and his brother Ian, whom Archie hired for the purchasing department in 1986.

111

ROBERT FOORD
COMES ON BOARD

Tom Foord acknowledges that he might have considered easing his self-imposed rule against hiring family earlier had his youngest son, Robert, indicated an interest in working at Kal. Robert had been exposed to tires most of his life. As children, Robert and his sister, Janet, thought it fun to ride on the conveyer belt in the Vernon warehouse. But to Tom's regret, Robert had been mostly dismissive of the idea of working for Kal.

What frustrated Tom about the decision so much was that Robert increasingly showed qualities that Tom would value in a Kal employee. Even in high school, Robert demonstrated a confident intelligence and adventurous curiosity reminiscent of Tom himself in his youth. An athlete on his way to becoming an accomplished skier, mountain biker and outdoorsman, Robert's enthusiasm for those pursuits, and a disinterest in tires and Kal — both of which had defined Tom's life — became a continuing source of friction between father and son. Robert wasn't sure what he wanted to do, he told his father, but he was pretty sure it wasn't going to involve tires — or Kal.

Archie, as much a friend of the family as he was a Kal executive, had known Robert since he was a teen. He worried that stubbornness and a fierce sense of independence, characteristics Tom and Robert share, would further drive a wedge between them. At Tom's request, Archie agreed to intervene. "I wanted to get Robert away from the albatross of his father hanging around his neck," says Archie.

Aware that Robert hoped to travel after he graduated from high school in 1976, Archie persuaded him to take the job at Kal's associate dealer store in Watson Lake on the Alaska Highway in the Yukon. "Archie sent me up north, to see if the experience would change how I felt about the business," Robert says. "But in my interest, he thought I could make buckets of money to go off and see the world, to get that out of my system."

Robert never considered the job as anything but temporary. At the end of the summer, using the money he made at Watson Lake, he went traveling in Europe with a high school friend. He returned home a year later to enroll in university, but chose an alternative to Kal to earn tuition money; a diver, he spent summers working on a project to eradicate milfoil, an invasive aquatic plant that threatened a number of B.C. lakes.

Twenty-three when he graduated from Simon Fraser University in Vancouver in 1981, Robert worked at the environmental job for the summer, at a ski shop in the winter, then indulged his wanderlust once more, traveling throughout Southeast Asia, then on to Australia. In Perth, he worked nights in a bar and days in a maternity hospital laundry to finance more travel in Asia. "For a guy who doesn't have any kids, I sure washed my fair share of diapers," he says.

Robert returned to Canada in 1986 and went to work for a stock promoter on the Vancouver Stock Exchange for eight months. Tom, no stranger to the excitement and financial attractions of the stock market, despaired of Robert ever joining Kal.

Not for the first time, Robert surprised his father. He became increasingly disenchanted with flogging stock. "I wasn't getting any younger," Robert says. "It was time to give Kal Tire a try. It wasn't exactly a big leap into the unknown, and I told myself that if I didn't like it I could always move on to something else."

He was a more mature 29-year-old in 1987 when he says he came to terms with working in his father's considerable shadow. "I was attracted and reluctant at the same time," he confesses. "You're the boss's son, but you try to gain the respect and credibility of others though your actions, not on the basis of your name."

As had been the case when Tom hired his son-in-law Ken Finch seven years earlier, Robert did not get a "family" pass. Following the Columbia Tire purchase, Kal had begun to consolidate its Vancouver-area inventory storage by moving stock from the old Advanx Tire dormitory-cum-warehouse under the Port Mann bridge into the bigger Columbia building on Annacis Island.

You're the boss's son, but you try to gain the respect and credibility of others through your actions, not on the basis of your name.

Opposite: Tom and Robert Foord in San Pedro de Atacama, on a visit to operations in nearby Antofagasta, Chile, 1999. **Above:** Robert Foord joined his father's company in 1987, starting out working in the warehouse on Annacis Island.

To make better use of the space, Kal planned to install a system called Narrow Aisle that featured special forklifts whose articulating forks turned 90 degrees to the left or right while the truck itself remained centred. Robert worked on the project to integrate the system.

After the completion of that job, Robert was transferred to the Langley store where he worked in sales and service. Being newly committed, he found, made a difference, even if the job still meant changing tires and rolling around under trucks. "It was hard physical labour," he says of his year in Langley. "But looking back on it now, I enjoyed it. This time it was a decision I had made."

After Langley, he spent a year and a half as an assistant manager in North Vancouver, and another year and a half as a salesman in Vancouver. But he wasn't yet entirely comfortable at Kal. It would have been impossible to hide his last name, so Robert had never tried. But he worried that it might look as though he was being given special treatment. "He found that his last name was a bigger problem than a plus," says Archie. "He wanted to be his own person, but was frustrated that he couldn't escape being the boss's son. I suggested he go to Edmonton. Nobody knew Tom there; Tom's a B.C. guy."

The move worked. Robert spent two years working with Robert Kehler in the Edmonton Yellowhead Trail store, then three years as the corporate salesman for Alberta, followed by another year managing the McKnight Boulevard store in Calgary. When Gary Morris retired as Kal's vice-president of sales, Robert moved back to Vernon to replace him, now confident that his performance justified his promotion.

As was standard practice for vice-presidents at Kal, Robert attended all the senior managers' meetings as part of the executive team that included his father. To the relief of Archie Stroh and Ken Finch especially, any differences between Robert and Tom seemed to have been forgotten.

In 1998, now a highly valued executive with experience across the company's operations, Robert became the second Foord to be a partner in Kal.

AN ASSOCIATE DECISION

Not everyone that Kal targeted as an associate was immediately attracted to the idea. Doug Barr, who had opened his tire store in 1979 in Fort St. John, on the Peace River in northeastern B.C., experienced an immediate business boom, went into debt during the recession of the early 1980s, then dug himself out. His business was prospering again in 1984 when Tom and Archie suggested he join Kal as an associate. Doug figured he was already getting a maximum discount from suppliers so what Kal was offering had few benefits.

Tom and Archie, however, pitched the intangibles that Kal Tire offered: the benefits of an association with a company with an excellent reputation; access to systems ranging from accounts receivable and engineering; and financial assistance with real estate and transportation. Doug says the fervour of Tom's description of Kal's work ethic and dedication to excellence won him over.

Doug became convinced over the next two years that he'd made the right move as Kal surpassed his expectations. "As soon as we were accepted as associates, Kal asked 'What can we do to help you succeed?'" Doug says. "They immediately embraced us and were there with whatever we needed. They provided us with motivation to be leaders rather than followers."

Kal also offered more tangible support. Chief financial officer Larry Wynn set up the bookkeeping at Doug's store to be compatible with Kal's; Ken Finch, vice-president of stores, assisted on the construction plans for a new store; Kal's real estate specialist John Blunt helped scout a location in town while Carey Hull oversaw its look and layout.

At first, Doug admits, he thought the new modern-looking outlet was out of its element in the bush on the fringe of town. But he soon recognized he'd been right to accept the Kal team's advice. "We were pioneers," says Doug. "Our store became the place to grow around. Soon everybody was located there, including a huge new Rona store, a casino and two new car dealerships. The town actually grew around us."

A NEW ADMAN TAKES THE REINS

The Vernon Men's Club was founded in 1913 as a place where local businessmen could meet socially. Over the years, it had never been overly popular with many women in town. Husbands who dropped in for a drink, a game of pool or a Friday night poker game on occasion weren't seen until the next morning. Before the club disbanded in the late 1990s, Archie admits to playing more games of pool there than perhaps he should have. And Tom indulged his love of poker at the club before he swore off the game. "There were times that both my wife and Tom's wife would have happily blown the place up," Archie confesses.

The club nonetheless had its place in Kal's history. Tom and Archie knew Gary Morris through the club, for instance; after they hired him as a salesman, he went on to become vice-president of sales. The Vernon Men's Club was also how they knew Wayne Kinghorn, the proprietor of a Vernon auto glass business. In 1986, Wayne shuttered the struggling operation and went traveling with his wife for a couple of years. When he returned, he approached Kal for a job.

Archie, who thought Wayne would make a good advertising manager, wasn't bothered by his lack of experience in the field. Tom Serviss hadn't known anything about advertising either, Archie reasoned, yet he'd learned on the fly, and gone on to help make Tom Foord and Kal household names. Given that success, Archie didn't see much risk in hiring Wayne to replace Tom Serviss who left Kal in 1988.

Although the hiring seemed inconsistent with Kal's effort to adopt more professional operating practices, Wayne was soon justifying the decision by upgrading his qualification for his job. For his first three years at Kal, he spent every long weekend on Vancouver Island taking advertising courses presented by some of Toronto's leading professionals in the field.

The results for the rest of Wayne's tenure in the job were palpable. When he retired in 2010, he had become a skilled advertising executive who'd spent 20 years at Kal, leaving an advertising and promotions program that helped Kal advance into retail markets. Another of Wayne's legacies at Kal was his son Michael, who joined the company just as Wayne retired. Michael has since been putting his expertise in the digital world to use by helping Kal make the transition to the "New Economy" era of the Internet.

Opposite: Doug Barr, who owned his own tire store in Fort St. John, was invited by Tom and Archie Stroh to join the Kal Tire team in 1984 as an associate. **Above:** Wayne Kinghorn, former proprietor of an auto glass company, joined Kal Tire as advertising manager, circa 1988.

CLOSING THE DECADE ON A HIGH

The Kal that Wayne Kinghorn joined in 1988 was a significantly different company from the one that had greeted his predecessor in 1982. While it remained dedicated to its small-town British Columbia roots and values, Kal was rapidly outgrowing the description "small." It had taken over three independent chains, moved into Vancouver and onto Vancouver Island, and expanded into Alberta. By 1988, it had 49 stores, 11 associate outlets and an active mining-tire division.

Archie Stroh characterizes the 1980s as "The Learning Decade." The recession had imposed on Kal the discipline to become a leaner, more efficient organization. Simultaneously paring down while restructuring to grow, Kal hadn't had much in the way of a guidebook or users' manual. Yet it had introduced the zone manager concept as an ongoing organizing and operating structure.

Executives like Ken Finch, Larry Wynn, Bruce Cantalope, Richard Hamilton and Gary Morris had joined Tom and Archie to build an energetic management team that had spearheaded growth. They'd injected discipline into Kal's operations, enabling it to initiate and cope with its dramatic expansion. And there were clear indications that measures such as tighter inventory control, more efficient distribution, and better training of personnel were having the desired impact. Kal's sales topped $120 million.

When Wayne Kinghorn was hired as advertising manager, Archie told him: "We're starting to polish the apple." Now it had done the polishing. What's more, the company had managed to do it without sacrificing the entrepreneurial flair that had been Kal's stock-in-trade for 27 years.

One consequence was that Tom Foord, Kal's unassuming patriarch, was increasingly in demand by interviewers seeking his secret in founding a business juggernaut. Typically, he shrugged and pointed out that there was no silver bullet or royal road. The secret of Kal's success, he indicated, was simply good citizenship. The company culture had evolved around the central principles of being needed, maintaining mutual trust with its suppliers and customers, providing better service than competitors, and seizing every opportunity it encountered in order to improve and grow.

Given how well it had all worked, Tom, 67 at the end of the decade, saw no reason that Kal wouldn't continue to thrive following the same formula as it headed into the 1990s.

Given how well it had all worked, Tom, 67 at the end of the decade, saw no reason that Kal wouldn't continue to thrive following the same formula as it headed into the 1990s.

CHAPTER SIX:

MANAGING GROWTH

(THE 1990s)

ANATOMY OF AN ACQUISITION

In any business whose participants often share suppliers and contend for the same markets, secrets are hard to keep, and the tire industry is especially notorious for gossip. But even Kal's well-informed executives were surprised in 1991 when they learned that creditors were ready to call in the debts and shut down Tire Town, Kal's toughest competitor in Alberta.

The owners of Tire Town founded the company in 1959 and built it into a chain of 33 stores, four retread plants and three distribution centres in the province. To outward appearances, the company was thriving. It boasted 350 or so employees and sales of $95 million. Yet in actuality, it had been teetering toward bankruptcy.

Wishing insolvency on competitors was hardly part of the culture Tom Foord had bred at Kal. But in the event that a rival was about to disappear, Kal was naturally interested in competing for its business. The possibility of buying Tire Town's assets immediately rose to the top of Kal's agenda.

To the irrepressible Archie Stroh, the decision to boost Kal's sales by $95 million was a no-brainer. Hadn't Kal spent the 1980s preparing for such an opportunity by learning how to operate as a large chain? Its staff was now better trained, its stores better managed, and concepts such as the zone manager system had injected business discipline into Kal. At the time, it operated 50 stores, a handful of retread operations and a distribution system that operated out of efficient warehouses, and it generated sales of about $145 million annually.

Ken Finch, on the other hand, was more cautious. He had initiated many of Kal's management improvements, but was aware that its operations were still far from perfect. He was also mindful of time and effort involved in integrating acquisitions. Merging such things as inventory and accounting systems, and rationalizing a new workforce with Kal's, could be a major distraction. It wasn't as though Kal was overstocked with managers, after all; most were already working full-bore running the business Kal already had.

Kal's partners, all members of senior management, met in a marathon session to weigh the pros and cons of bidding for Tire Town. Ultimately they agreed that opportunities to virtually double in size were rare. At 4:30 a.m., Archie informed the creditors' committee that Kal would be making a bid to take over Tire Town.

Kal's proposal was unconventional. Tire Town wasn't technically in bankruptcy, which meant Kal was dealing with a committee of creditors rather than a trustee. Kal wanted the committee's assurance that small creditors wouldn't lose out to larger ones. "It took a lot of persuading to get them all to agree to that idea," Archie says. "We felt that the small creditors shouldn't suffer and that the bigger ones could wait. They finally came to terms with it, so we went ahead."

Opposite: In the 1990s, Kal prepared for future opportunities by learning how to staff and operate a rapidly expanding chain of stores that included outlets at Westbank and Weyburn.

Tire Town turned out to be the most ambitious of Kal Tire's takeovers, and the swiftest. On Friday night the creditors shut the stores. On Monday Tire Town's outlets reopened under Kal Tire's ownership. Among the most surprised people were some of the 350 Tire Town employees. They'd been unaware of Tire Town's troubles, and showed up for work only to discover that they had a new employer.

Doug Starling, whose father had worked at Columbia Tire when Kal bought that company, sympathized with the Tire Town employees: "They thought everything was fine, and then all of a sudden this big black cloud from Vernon descended on them. Emotions and insecurities ran high. Because Kal Tire is a culture unto itself, there was a perception that we were a controlling company, and the employees were very, very nervous."

As Ken Finch had cautioned, Kal's challenge after doubling in size to 100 stores in one leap became a matter of absorbing Tire Town into Kal Tire with the least disruption so that it could begin contributing. And as he'd predicted, the digestion process put demands on Kal's entire executive team.

Those involved in the integration couldn't help noticing at least one cultural difference between Tire Town and Kal. The Alberta company's employees didn't have the same dedication to service that Kal employees took for granted. "Tire Town was in the retail business and we were in the commercial business," says Robert Kehler. "They didn't sell the same services we did. For us, it was all about service, but they were always quick to close the stores early."

Tom Foord was also quick to spot operational waste when visiting a Tire Town warehouse on a day when it was 40 degrees below. He was astonished to see workers in shirtsleeves. He ordered the thermostat turned down from 70 degrees. "A Kal Tire warehouse is 50 degrees, and you put on a sweater," he fumed. "Tires don't need to be kept warm!"

The volume of product in Tire Town's warm warehouses also caught Kal's team by surprise, especially since Tire Town itself wasn't exactly sure of what it had in stock. "They carried far too much inventory — tons and tons of it that didn't sell," Robert Kehler says. "From the moment we put in our computer system we understood their business far better."

Rationalizing two managements, which is never easy in mergers, was complicated by the refusal of some of Tire Town's staff to adopt Kal's work habits. "By the time we finished straightening out the mess, none of the senior executives were left," says Tom Foord. "They didn't want to be bothered with us. Then the second tier management thought we were too tough to work with and they left. We ended up with about four hundred new team members, but we had human resource problems for quite a while."

To establish the bond between stores and head office, which was also crucial to spreading the Kal Tire way to new employees, Bruce Cantalope, vice-president of stores, made sure he visited every Tire Town outlet — building relationships, helping with training programs, and generally encouraging cooperation among Kal and Tire Town employees.

Archie Stroh went further: he moved to Edmonton in October 1991. Except for a week at home at Christmas, he stayed until April. He viewed Kal's visitation and training approach as imperial in nature, a means of spreading its culture. "If you're going to have a branch business you have to run it like the Romans did," he says. "The Romans trained their people and sent them out as true Romans who really understood what Rome was all about. I also knew that in order to transfer Kal Tire to other places, I had to know what that market was all about."

Kal used the zone concept to advantage. It placed its best managers in former Tire Town stores where they worked to instill Kal values in the staff. "When we took it over, a lot of Tire Town's store managers could talk the talk but couldn't walk the walk," says Larry Wynn. "The zone concept really moved things forward and got stores up and running and making a profit much faster."

The knowledge flow wasn't all one way, as Tire Town had some things to teach Kal too. It had a retail-oriented operating model, and experience with mechanical repairs, both of which were more advanced than Kal's. Kal, of course, was only too happy to adopt new ways to serve tire-buyers wherever it found them. "We didn't keep most of their managers," Robert Kehler notes, "but we retained a lot of good people, and we started learning the retail business — and what had worked or hadn't worked in that particular environment. Tire Town majored in the mechanical repair business, so we had to learn more about mechanics, what to do, and what to stay away from — like tune-ups. Tune-ups take a long time, and there's a high rate of customer dissatisfaction."

Not everything in the integration process went according to plan. Initially, Kal had seen merit in continuing to operate Tire Town and Kal outlets as separate brands. Tire Town had invested heavily in advertising and marketing over 30 years to establish its brand. Kal hoped to leverage that investment. "We'd seen it as our chance to have two brands," says Archie. "But guys became confused about just who they were working for."

Worse, it was a money-losing proposition. When Larry Wynn discovered after a year that he was $1 million short of the revenue projection he'd made to the bank, Kal dropped the two-brand idea and shuttered the less successful Tire Town stores, converting the rest to outlets bearing the trusted Kal Tire logo.

While most of the activity triggered by the Tire Town purchase took place at the store level in Alberta, there were ramifications at head office in Vernon, too. Kal hired 16 new staff to deal with the increased workload. Much of it involved either reconciling hundreds of new accounts from Tire Town customers who insisted they'd already paid their bills, or correcting payments credited to the wrong account. The group assigned to the task wore name tags and proudly called themselves The Herd. "Nobody was prepared for the avalanche of business and paperwork," says Lynda Torvik, one of three Herd members still at Kal. "We just winged it."

Throughout the merger process, Kal tried to maintain programs that Bruce Cantalope and Gary Morris had designed to promote Kal as a brand name. Bruce developed the VIP program that sent cards to Kal's commercial customers such as truck companies and their employees, offering discounts on retail services and products. Bruce had the cards mailed to their homes, so the customers' spouses would see them, adding to Kal's name recognition.

Another promotional program, developed by Robert Kehler, was designed to re-emphasize Kal's superior service. Top Gun Service was centred on winter tire changeovers and appealed to the competitive nature of Kal's service staff. The idea was that teams of three or four staff trained and timed themselves to see who was fastest at swapping customers' tires from summer to winter models. The competitions were played up as events that attracted customers and the press.

GIVING UP ON GOODYEAR

A tradition at Kal almost as old as the company itself is the Monday morning meeting at which senior managers bring each other up-to-date on their area of the business and discuss new ideas being considered. A frequent topic of conversation has always been the latest status of supplier-dealer alliances, always fraught with turmoil in the tire business.

Essentially, manufacturers supply product to dealers who mark up the price to reflect the service they deliver installing and maintaining the tires on customers' vehicles. Suppliers also have their own single-brand stores that compete with dealers, but they tend to concentrate on retail markets and leave the more difficult-to-serve commercial and OTR markets to dealers. Suppliers, however, have occasionally sought to bypass dealers to sell to the commercial and OTR markets directly.

In the mid-1980s, another topic of discussion at Kal's meetings had been the possible purchase of Crown Tire, a major OTR dealer based in Edmonton. At the time, Kal was a Bridgestone dealer. Bridgestone, however, had knocked Kal out of the running when it purchased Crown in 1987. "I knew if it really wanted Crown, Bridgestone could simply go ahead and get it," Tom says. "There was no way we could compete."

Rather than continue as a Bridgestone dealer competing with Crown, Kal had subsequently resigned itself to maintaining a relationship with Goodyear, which Tom thought was a reasonably sound arrangement. Even when Bridgestone made Crown Tire its exclusive OTR dealer in Western Canada, Tom remained confident that Kal had Goodyear's support in the marketplace.

Following the integration of Tire Town into Kal in the early 1990s, management had been looking anew for expansion opportunities in Alberta. One had been another Goodyear dealer. But before Kal could act, it got a shock when Goodyear's president, whom Tom considered a friend, flew to Tom's winter vacation home in Palm Springs, California, for a golf game and a business meeting. Over drinks, the executive dropped a bombshell: Goodyear, he told Tom, had just bought an interest in Fountain Tire, a Goodyear dealership in Alberta.

Effectively, instead of expanding, Kal would now be competing in some markets with Goodyear, its major supplier. Tom did his best to hide his devastation. To Archie's disbelief, Tom even maintained enough composure to show up for his tee-time the following morning with the Goodyear president. To Archie, it was like playing a round with Judas. "I would have thumped the guy," he says, "and I definitely wouldn't have been playing golf with him." Nor was Archie impressed that Tom sent the Goodyear executive a gift a few years later when he retired. "He sure as hell wouldn't have received a gift from me," he says. "But that's the way Tom is."

Although Kal remained a Goodyear dealer under the new president, the relationship grew rockier. Goodyear agreed to honour its agreement to supply Kal Tire's existing Alberta stores — in Edmonton, Grande Prairie and Hinton. But it refused to ship product to any new stores Kal opened in the province. Goodyear's intransigence crimped Kal's expansion plans in Alberta. Kal stayed with Goodyear for another year and a half, says Tom, but Kal's growth in its existing markets was now limited to British Columbia.

Tom Foord, as sanguine as ever about the events that had befallen Kal through no fault of its own, blames Goodyear's position on corporate politics. "Every new president has to make a name for himself," he shrugs, "and the fastest way to do it is to make changes. Whether the changes were any good or not was open to question. The only thing we knew was that in three years, there'd be another new president."

And there was. But unfortunately, Tom was unable to educate him to the realities of the business: instead the new man parachuted into the job tried to talk Tom into handling Kelly Springfield tires, Goodyear's second-line product, offering Kal exclusive rights in B.C. Tom felt the offer was insulting to Kal. For one thing, the Kelly Springfield line didn't include mining tires. "It took three more meetings to convince him it was a ridiculous idea because they didn't have any of the products we needed," says Tom.

Tom's refusal to take on Goodyear's secondary product line may have turned out to be a bad idea in the short term. Although Goodyear left the Kelly Springfield offer on the table, it informed Tom — by special delivery mail rather than in person — that Kal's 20-year relationship with Goodyear was otherwise over. "I felt sick," says Tom. "The problem was I had no alternative in mind."

Never one to cave in the face of setbacks, Tom displayed yet again the resilience that had served him so well in business. He also proved the value of the respect he showed to friends and foes alike that had so frustrated Archie when he'd kept the golf date with the Goodyear president. Over the years, Tom's effortless good nature had attracted a wide network of friends, allies and admirers. Though reluctant to appear to be using personal relationships, the looming debacle at Kal called for desperate measures. Swallowing his pride, Tom made a call to an old friend, Bruce McNichol, the former president of Bridgestone Canada.

That phone call was probably the most important one Tom made in 40 years of business. It set the stage for Kal's emergence from a successful regional company to a leading tire distributor in North America.

CONNECTING WITH BRIDGESTONE

The conversation with Bruce was brief. After telling his friend of Goodyear's action, he wondered whether Bridgestone would be interested in Kal's business. An incredulous Bruce McNichol responded as Tom had hoped he would. "He said to me, 'Would they be interested? You bet they would,'" Tom says.

Sticking to his belief that he was in a better bargaining position if a supplier approached him than if he went hat-in-hand to the supplier, Tom asked Bruce to quietly drop the word that Kal Tire might be leaving Goodyear, and there was a chance it would be available. Within an hour he had a response. Ed Hyjek, president of Bridgestone Canada, called to set up a meeting with Tom for the next morning in Palm Springs.

The meeting stretched into three days of golf and negotiations. Tom insisted during the talks that Kal be permitted to take over Crown Tire's 15 Alberta stores, which Bridgestone had outbid it for in 1987. Bridgestone happily agreed. "It turned out that Bridgestone hadn't done that well with Crown Tire," says Tom. "They knew that we were the people who had what it took to run branches."

The negotiations concluded in 1993 with Kal buying everything Bridgestone owned in B.C. and Alberta. Four years later, in 1997, Kal Tire also acquired James Tire in Saskatchewan and Manitoba from Bridgestone. Altogether, the Crown/James purchase added 31 locations, including 18 retail outlets, seven associate stores, three Bandag retread shops and three warehouses. An additional 136 employees from Crown and related operations boosted Kal's total to 1,500 people in 131 outlets. The acquisition also added new markets. James Tire in Manitoba and Sasken Tire in Saskatchewan, which were part of the deal, satisfied Kal's quest for an entry into the farm-tire market.

Opposite: Archie Stroh (third from left) at a meeting with Goodyear in the mid-1970s — throughout the years the relationship between Kal Tire and Goodyear was at times tense and mistrustful, as it was between many dealers and suppliers in the industry. Above: A newspaper ad from 1993 announces a Kal Tire open house.

When you put your trust into the hands of a supplier, and they put their trust in you, you're both vulnerable.

As good as it all looked, Tom and the Kal management team remained wary. They had experienced enough setbacks to recognize that any new relationship in the tire business can be fraught with sudden reverses. "When you put your trust into the hands of a supplier, and they put their trust in you, you're both vulnerable," says Tom. "A dealer can sell out to a competing supplier, and suddenly the supplier has no outlets for his product. You've got to be completely honest and transparent with each other. As in any important relationship, you earn trust through constant communication, and recognizing the importance of any issue that affects you both."

It took just three meetings with Bridgestone's top executives in Tokyo and in North America to reassure Tom and the Kal team that their concern was unnecessary. "Although the Japanese are traditionally very slow to show trust," says Tom, "they could see that there were no hidden agendas. From the start of our relationship they planned their own growth in a way that wouldn't conflict with our plans."

Kal's partners, and Tom in particular, were especially gratified by the way the deal had been handled. In an industry plagued by mistrust on both sides, the transaction had more closely resembled a meeting of minds. The respectful modesty that defined Kal's corporate character was no accident. It was a proxy for Tom's own ethos, woven into the fabric of Kal from the outset.

Bridgestone, Tom believed, was a kindred spirit. Like him, it saw merit in planning well into the future. "The big American companies changed presidents regularly, and each president had his own agenda," says Tom. "But the Japanese company thought in the long term, not just about what was going to happen financially the next day."

Benefits from the new partnership with Bridgestone accrued to Kal almost immediately. The Crown purchase, including James and Sasken, closed in March 1998, adding revenue of $27 million to Kal's own 1997 revenue of $239 million. There was every reason to expect 1998 sales to surpass $350 million. After coming so close to disaster, that prospect elated Tom Foord. "We just blossomed," he says.

Prior to the Kal deal, Bridgestone had lagged in the earthmover tire market. "Goodyear had it all, because we had got it for them," says Tom. But it didn't take Kal long to reverse that. Within 18 months, it had sold enough Bridgestone tires to make Bridgestone number one in B.C. and Alberta.

In the end, says Tom, his fundamental belief that success comes from making yourself needed had once more proved true. "I sometimes think of it as luck," he says, "but the fact is, if you build a business by being needed, these things will happen."

WHEN IN JAPAN

Kal's association with Bridgestone raised a concern that Kal had previously never faced — its executives would be interacting with a Japanese-owned company. They were anxious that, because of cultural differences, they might inadvertently offend their new business partner.

The potential for making a faux pas while trying to communicate in Japanese, for instance, had been related to them through the (possibly apocryphal) tale of an executive who famously used his newly learned Japanese to say what he thought was "Good evening, ladies and gentlemen," only to learn he'd actually said "Good evening, water closets and urinals."

To prepare itself, Kal hired experts to deliver a crash course in Japanese customs and culture to senior managers. The sessions with professional coaches acquainted the Canadian executives with such things as the importance to the Japanese of first impressions, proper bowing procedures, and the etiquette of giving and receiving gifts. Pocketing an offered business card, Kal's managers learned, was considered disrespectful in Japanese business culture; the Japanese expected recipients of a card to receive it in both hands.

Some of the nuances of Japanese culture were more difficult for Kal's managers to grasp. The Japanese aversion to saying no, for example, required some adjustment. Kal's people were more accustomed to straightforward business dealings that could at times be viewed as aggressive by the Japanese. Axioms such as "the nail that sticks out gets hammered down" captured the spirit of Japan's more collective approach to work, but didn't resonate strongly with Kal employees who prided themselves on standing apart from the crowd.

The Japanese term *kaizen*, on the other hand, had instant resonance. The word means continuous improvement and is applied to both business and life in Japan.

To Kal, kaizen described Kal's philosophy and operating objectives perfectly.

SPREADING THE
KAL CULTURE

Kal Tire's growth in the mid- to late 1990s was evidence that it had acquired the flexibility to manage through downturns and rebound with a high-growth expansion. The Tire Town and Bridgestone purchases gave it 131 stores, vaulting Kal into the role of the biggest independent tire dealer in Western Canada. But the stunning growth presented its own challenges. Chief among them was a familiar problem: how to instill the Kal culture in new employees and managers, many of whom had come to Kal from another company.

Much of the responsibility for the task fell to Archie Stroh, vice-president and general manager. To him, the answer was personal contact. It was the approach Tom had begun with at Kal and then nurtured throughout its history. But continuing a personal-contact approach at a company that had in only a few years doubled in size was daunting even for an executive of Archie's calibre. Nonetheless, for most of the spring and summer of 1998, he gave it his best shot. "When we bought James Tire in Manitoba and Sasken in Saskatchewan, I drove every road in their territories," Archie recalls. "I went into every store and talked to every guy. By the time I got home I had put a face on Kal Tire for these people."

Archie's tour gave new employees and managers a chance to meet one of Kal's most effusive senior managers in person. On his "walkabout," Archie looked for the motivating characteristic of employees he met. "For some people it's the future, for some it's family," he says. "But mostly it's their pride; people want to be proud of the job they do, and to be appreciated, respected and thanked. I always gave them respect in spades."

The familiarization tour was also an opportunity to evaluate the markets that Kal was now entering through its acquisitions. "I had a real good picture of what those communities and those markets were all about," he says. Although pleased for the most part, he also spotted places where Kal would have to adjust its usual method of serving a region. In Winnipeg, for example, it spent $850,000 renovating a store, only to discover the store's main clientele — commercial fleets — couldn't have cared less and Kal would probably have been better off operating out of an old warehouse with a fleet of service trucks. "Its commercial customers were too large and self-sustaining to come to the store," says Archie. "Winnipeg was like Toronto; you go to their yard, they don't come to yours."

> *For some people it's the future, for some it's family. But mostly it's their pride; people want to be proud of the job they do, and to be appreciated, respected and thanked. I always gave them respect in spades.*

THE "RETAILIFICATION"
OF KAL

Following the Crown Tire purchase, Kal expected there would be the occasional Crown Tire outlet competing with a nearby Kal Tire outlet. Selecting which to keep was a matter of scrutinizing the books to determine the most profitable of them. When Robert Kehler saw the results of the audits, however, he was shocked at the fickleness of the local market. "To our surprise we discovered that some of the customers we thought had been loyal to us had been doing business with Crown, too," he says. "We had to take a close look at what mistakes we'd been making that drove them to do that."

Reminded of the vicissitudes of the competitive retail market, Kal Tire re-examined its business model. It had built its reputation over 40 years selling mainly commercial tires to truckers, and off-road specialized tires to natural resource companies like mines and forestry companies. Seventy percent of Kal's business was commercial. Management concluded that it needed assistance to develop strategies to attack the other 30 percent, the retail segment.

Tom and his team turned once again to Tom's friend Les Schwab, whose Portland, Oregon-based chain was the leading independent retail tire dealer in the U.S. Les's stores featured showrooms stacked with tires and after-market wheels that customers could actually touch and see.

Les impressed on Kal the need for patience. The retail tire business, he pointed out, is more competitive than the commercial one, but slow at the outset. In his view, only through consistent service could Kal build sustainable momentum. "We were kind of pumped when we returned to Vernon," says Robert Kehler, one of those who'd been on the Portland fact-finding mission. "We all knew what Les had done. Now that we had seen it, we didn't see why we couldn't duplicate it in Canada."

Kal already had the requisite fundamentals to work with. In addition to its experienced team of tire men, entrepreneurial leaders and a culture with a baked-in enthusiasm and energy, it viewed business as a long-view proposition, not a quick profit-grab. Moreover, its 131 stores across Western Canada gave it a stable platform on which to build a retail business that would serve a new cohort of customers who drove cars and light trucks instead of 18-wheelers and earthmovers.

Nor was the retail tire business entirely foreign to Kal. Edmonton-based Tire Town had been primarily a retail chain when Kal bought it in 1991, and Kal had continued operating it that way. In 1995, Robert Kehler had advocated strengthening Kal's thrust into the retail market, and the company had done so in a big way: it opened its largest, most costly outlet yet in Edmonton.

The store's location, on a main thoroughfare, demonstrated Kal's ambition to attract car and light truck business. Its scale, though, was distinctly un-Kal-like. It featured 10 service bays. Its 4,000-square-foot showroom on its own was the size of many Kal stores. Along with specialty wheels and accessories on display, its racks were stocked with 2,500 tires. "The most Kal had ever had in a showroom at one time was 20 tires," Robert says.

Robert had been determined that the store would not suffer due to under-funding. But he concedes that the experiment's costs were incongruous with Kal's usual thrift, and that it raised the occasional eyebrow at the Monday morning management meetings. "Edmonton was the most expensive store we'd ever had," he says. "We never dreamed we'd be paying over $20,000 in rent for a building. Believe me it was a struggle; we thought we'd lose money for years."

Opposite: Archie Stroh and Bruce Cantalope spoke to participants at a company team meeting about the "Kal Tire way" — one of their primary missions was to instill the Kal culture in the new employees they inherited when Kal Tire bought other companies. **This page, clockwise from right:** By the 1990s Kal Tire's retail outlets were sporting a crisp, professional look. A Les Schwab retail outlet — Les Schwab was a friend and mentor of Tom Foord's. The new look of a Kal Tire store.

IF Y
WE

To
WE
FOR A
BUSINE
You m

E SELL IT...
GUARANTEE IT!

KAL TIRE

Our Customers...

RE RESPONSIBLE
L ASPECTS OF THE
SS WE DO WITH YOU.

st be satisfied. **KAL TIRE**

The store actually turned a profit, albeit a small one, in its first year. That persuaded Kal to keep pushing to figure out the retail end of its business. Management had identified Carey Hull as a good candidate to spearhead its thrust. Carey had managed a retail oriented store for Tire Town. He stayed on at Kal in 1992 to manage its Calgary warehouse. In his newly created role of retail coordinator, he moved to Vernon.

On his initial visits to Kal's stores, Carey concluded that most were too tightly focused on truck and OTR customers at the expense of the car-driving public. "Commercial was close to the hearts of these guys," he says, "and they didn't want to deal with retail. Commercial was where they had their biggest sales volume. They didn't want to stop what they were doing to look after a retail customer and make very little money on car tires."

Carey responded with a program to spiff up stores to give them more general appeal, and to develop more of a retail sensibility among store managers. As part of the program, he insisted on moving truck, farm and construction tires from the front of the store to the back shop. In their place, only passenger tires would be displayed. Commercial customers, he reasoned, knew what Kal sold, "but retail customers don't like to be surrounded by heavy-duty truck tires when someone is working on their car."

Carey also reinforced the Kal brand. Its own posters emphasizing service replaced ads supplied by tire manufacturers that focused on product.

He repainted store interiors in Kal's beige, blue and orange corporate colours to give outlets a consistent look across the chain. He also replaced long counters in reception areas with smaller, less intimidating podium-style sales centres that encouraged one-on-one contact with customers.

Kal had never paid much attention in the past to displaying tires. Les Schwab's belief that retail buyers like to see what they're buying, however, changed that thinking. Kal began stacking showrooms with racks of clean passenger tires. Salespeople could point out what they were selling and customers could touch them. For good measure, an array of custom wheels added a touch of glitter. As Kal Tire became more deeply committed to its retail business, stores added mechanical services, free brake and tire pressure inspections, wheel alignment and items such as windshield wipers.

Still, the "retailification" process had to overcome some old habits. Kal's reception-area staff had traditionally dressed casually. Back-shop workers, naturally, wore old clothes; handling tires, after all, was hardly a clean job. And for some, the dirt on their coveralls was almost a badge of the pride they took in their labour. Many old hands balked at first at the notion of uniforms bearing Kal's logo. They feared looking like the staff of a fast-food outlet.

Kal helped win them over by supplying free work clothes and by looking after the laundering. Kal also persuaded employees that it was in their interest to keep long hair and unkempt beards trimmed, and body piercings and tattoos covered up. Professional appearances helped assure customers that they were being well looked after. Kal reminded staff that these satisfied customers were crucial to Kal's health, and to their jobs.

Kal was soon able to offer hard evidence that its approach was working. "It took about a year for our new Edmonton store to make a bit of profit," says Robert Kehler, zone manager of Alberta at the time. "But within five years we were so successful that we moved all the commercial business out of it and ran it as a pure retail store. It turned out to be the best retail move we ever made."

THE AIMS: A COHERENT STATEMENT OF VALUES

Over 45 years, Kal Tire had evolved into a closely knit, high-energy organization with a flat structure overseen by a compact management team. Kal had a family component in a literal sense; it employed relatives of Tom Foord. But it was more inclined to use the term "family" in a figurative sense, characterizing the entire organization as the Kal family.

Inevitably, however, the familiarity that enabled Tom Foord and his senior managers to address every Kal employee by name became a casualty of growth. The Tire Town and Crown Tire purchases had added more than 500 people to the family. But while Kal asked new employees to embrace its culture and values, nobody had actually gone so far as to articulate exactly what the culture and values were.

Ironically, Kal's failure to do so was in a sense itself attributable to its culture. It had reveled in succeeding in the often rowdy tire business by relying at times on entrepreneurial derring-do or spontaneous decision-making based on instinct and intuition. And Kal was understandably reluctant to dampen that spirited enthusiasm.

Yet it was becoming apparent that as the financial stakes got bigger, and as its affairs were increasingly interwoven with more employees, customers and suppliers, the now very large company needed to encapsulate what it was, its aspirations, and guidelines for best achieving them. Unless Kal could explain coherently to itself what it was, Ken Finch believed, it risked losing focus on what it wanted to be and how to reach that objective. "For the first time," he says, "we were in danger of losing our way."

Professional appearances helped assure customers that they were being well looked after. These satisfied customers were crucial to Kal's health.

Above: Carey Hull, who managed the Tire Town warehouse, was hired by Kal Tire in 1992 to "retail-ify" its stores.

Kal's plain-spoken, hard-working management hadn't showed an inclination toward business fads or hiring consultants to help it run the company. But in the early 1990s, when Ken Finch flew to San Diego to hear a speech by Dr. W. Edwards Deming, a statistician whose genius is credited with reviving the Japanese economy after World War II, he was impressed enough to suggest that Archie Stroh catch one of Deming's addresses. Archie too found Deming's concepts fascinating. But the two Kal managers couldn't immediately identify how to employ Deming's theories and methods at Kal.

Seeking more input, they arranged for all the partners to fly to Dallas to hear Deming's address. This time, one of Deming's concepts got some traction. He rejected mission statements as unrealistic goals set by managers in ivory towers. "Instead, he talked at great length about the importance of articulating the aims of a company, and most importantly, to put them down on paper," says Ken. "And that's exactly what we proceeded to do."

Or tried to do. In fact, the partners had a difficult time when they sat down to determine precisely what Kal was all about. Ken Finch facilitated the exercise by suggesting they distill the challenge to answering a simple question: "When we are working at our best, what is it that makes us successful?" In answering, they slowly developed a list of core values of Kal that would become known as the AIMS.

The intent of the AIMS was to articulate a credo that expresses what Kal is in terms of how it thinks and acts. And as it turned out, the AIMS were relevant almost immediately. "At the time, expansion was a big topic," says Ken Finch. "Buying companies is easy; all you have to do is write a cheque. The hard part is what you do once you have them."

Putting dots on the map would have indicated where Kal had operations, he says, but all the disconnected dots wouldn't add up to anything that looked like a unified system and culture. "All those dots would just be a bunch of disconnected businesses that didn't share the same values. Until we could figure out how to spread our culture — and make it stick — we couldn't expand our business in any really meaningful way. As it stood at this point, we realized that our biggest weakness was that we were trying to reach beyond our grasp."

Individually and together, the management group thrashed out the AIMS and wrote them down. Archie spent weeks in the field talking to store managers and staff to get their feedback. "I probably drove managers nuts with my questions," he says. "A lot of what we were dealing with was theoretical. They're used to being more nuts and bolts."

Eventually, the distillation process reached the point where the team agreed that further changes were unnecessary. The AIMS document fulfilled the original objective. Kal felt it had consensually mapped its genetic makeup. It had defined itself and established a code for its continuing existence. But the test came when it set out to weave the values and principles in AIMS into the Kal fabric. And management was both relieved and gratified by the response it got. "Interestingly, people who had been around for years working shoulder to shoulder with us said, 'So that's what we're all about!'" says Archie.

In Ken Finch's view, the power of the AIMS isn't their uniqueness. In a literal sense, he acknowledges, some of them — such as always exceeding expectations — are actually unachievable. But they remain an elegantly simple guide to a way of thinking. "Most people who live an ethical life pretty much follow the AIMS principles," Ken says. "But it was important to get them down on paper and in our heads."

To Richard Hamilton, an original Kal Tire partner who retired in 1996, a major strength of the AIMS is that they're not goals or exhortations to do better. "When you reach a goal, that's it," he points out. "An AIM is an ongoing thing. To this day whenever I make a decision I think of the AIMS."

In addition to being drilled into the consciousness of every employee at hiring, AIMS are on the wall of every Kal Tire office, store, warehouse and retread plant. More than a mere reminder, they help the individual parts of Kal make sense as a whole. All the dots on a map indicating locations, for instance, are linked by the adherence of their personnel to the AIMS values. "The AIMS allowed us to expand in a way that made us stronger, not just bigger," says Ken. "We weren't at risk any more of losing our way."

THE AIMS

The AIMS, which define Kal's existence and values, appear on the wall of every Kal Tire operation:

1 Our aim is to earn the trust of our customers by providing them with a level of quality and value of both service and products that exceeds their expectations and exceeds that available from the competition.

2 Our aim is that the career of every team member is supported by quality leadership, training, and opportunities for advancement. Our people will work safely and have the ambition, enthusiasm and energy to be productive, efficient and contribute to an upbeat atmosphere in the workplace.

3 Our aim is to achieve a fair profit in all of our operations.

4 Our aim is to expand our company in a deliberate and balanced fashion for the purpose of strengthening our ability to serve the customer and provide a solid future for our people. However, our rate of expansion will not be beyond our ability to finance or manage to a consistent standard of quality.

5 Our aim is to conduct ourselves with honesty and integrity, being conscious of our image and with modest respect for our successes. Our image is defined by the conduct of each of us.

6 Our aim is to build long-term relationships with our suppliers based on competitiveness, value and mutual respect of objectives.

7 Our aim is to continually improve every aspect of our company, recognizing our responsibility to our customers, each other, our communities and the environment.

KAL TIRE 50/50 PARTNERSHIP

COMMITMENT

2009/10

LOCATION: 625   DATE: MAY 20/09

The Aims:

The Kal Tire Aims being constantly used as a guide.

All team members understand and accept the time demands of serving the public.

All Team Members will work safely.

People:

All team members will find and encourage the hiring of the best people available by selling the benefits of a career with Kal Tire.

All team members will coach new employees through their training so that they are able to contribute and represent the company in a manner consistent with the Aims.

Promotions and staffing levels will be based on ability and attitude.

Management and counter people will help with the service work, and service people will help with sales.

All team members will be actively involved in expense control.

Sales:

All team members will recognize that our greatest potential for improved profits is through increased sales.

Every new employee will receive sales training.

Everyone in the store will sell.

Image:

All team members will assist in maintaining a higher level of housekeeping in all areas of the store.

All will dress as per Kal Tire standards.

The personal appearance and conduct of everyone in the store will be consistent with the Aims.

Partners:

KAL TIRE
True Service.

THE 50/50 PARTNERSHIP

Facing a shortage of suitable managers to staff new stores during expansion in the 1970s, Tom Foord had introduced a program called the B Partnership. Under the plan, a manager had autonomy to operate the store under the Kal name as if it were his own. Along with the Kal brand, B Partners got the benefit of Kal's supply chain, could earn an interest in their stores, and received a share of its profits, provided the store met Kal's performance criteria. "I thought if they were like me, industrious, hard-working and honest, they would jump at the chance," Tom says of the B Partnership program.

Unhappily, the B Partnerships didn't perform as expected. Within a few years, Kal shut the program down. Tom concedes that his expectations may have been too high. Instead of developing as entrepreneurs, he says, the B Partners needed too much assistance from Kal's thinly staffed head office. "They had to be told and shown what to do, and that's not what we wanted."

But the situation left Kal a little embarrassed. While it claimed to feel responsible for employees in the workplace, Kal had no pension plan or program. Meanwhile, the difficulty of squaring business imperatives with social responsibilities had been driven home in the recession of the early 1980s. From a business standpoint, layoffs had been necessary to survive the recession. But management had been genuinely shaken by the impact the cutbacks had had on the families of employees. Many affected employees had had to survive on savings and unemployment insurance. Even if most of those workers laid off had been rehired, they'd had a glimpse into their future. In the absence of a pension plan, they'd be pretty much as financially hard-pressed when they retired.

To Ken Finch, the situation was hardly an endorsement of Kal's claimed social responsibility. "There was a moment when it became crystal clear to me that we needed to do something about this," he says. "I started looking farther down the road, and what I could see was a lot of good people working with their hands and making an average wage, and when they got to retirement age they wouldn't have anything put away. They might have a house, a truck and a boat, but no real money. I could see us starting to write out cheques because we felt a personal responsibility to Kal Tire people who were destitute after working all those years. That just wouldn't work."

While a pension plan made sense, finding the right program proved elusive. Kal's preference, reflecting its entrepreneurial roots, was a meritocratic program that tied promotions and compensation to performance while aligning employees' interests with Kal's. But there were no conventional plans that filled the bill. "Every one we looked at seemed to come with another problem," Ken says.

Recalling how close to the bone it had cut operations to survive during the downturn, he felt financing a conventional pension plan would put Kal at risk. "A company has to continue funding its pension whether it is profitable or not," he points out. "If we had another recession, we'd have the fixed cost of a pension fund acting like a heavy weight on the company."

In the end, Kal decided in 1987 to introduce the Base Plan. The Plan consists of individual employee RRSP accounts. The Base Plan is jointly funded by employees and Kal's stores. Employees contribute 2 percent of their gross pay and the company contributes 15 percent of the total profits of all Kal stores. The plan is compulsory for employees with two or more years of service and the fund is professionally managed so it will grow by the time it is needed by employees for retirement.

Some years later when reviewing the plan, Ken viewed profit sharing as a benefit Kal could promote to encourage employees to think of Kal as a career, not just a job. Accordingly, he explored ways that individual stores could not only fund the company-wide base plan and continue to share profits with store managers and assistants (as Kal's profit sharing plan had since 1987), but also more immediately reward store employees whose efforts were largely responsible for their individual stores' profits.

Opposite: A Kal Tire team member in Calgary shows a 2009 50/50 Partnership Commitment, an employee sharing plan that established Kal Tire as a leader in the industry.

The answer turned out to be to extend to all employees in the individual stores the profit-sharing program that had been in place for managers and assistants. Ken saw this next step, eventually labeled Team Share, as a program that encouraged a cooperative effort by all store employees to build their own store's profits. But while the idea worked conceptually, when Ken crunched the numbers to determine the percentage of store profits that Kal could realistically share with employees through the store plan, he came up with 47. "A plan called '47/53'," he says, "wasn't likely to fire up anybody's imagination."

The solution was obvious, if expensive: Kal boosted its contribution of store profits to the team in each store from 32 percent to 35 percent. Under Team Share, employees receive two-thirds of the profit share in cash and the rest is contributed to the individual employees' base profit-sharing accounts.

But the point was, when added to the 15 percent that Kal's stores division already contributed to the base profit sharing partnership, the increase to 35 percent gave employees 50 percent of the total amount of profit from stores. In 1995 the 50/50 partnership was born. "That jump of 3 percent has probably wound up costing us millions," Ken allows, "but it got people's attention. Team members, past and present, could see that the best people working at Kal Tire could wind up making more than some professionals."

Even so, Kal's traditional corporate discretion created an ironic predicament. Kal had historically been loath to reveal financial results, lest competitors, suppliers or customers use the information to gain a competitive advantage. Reluctance to disclose profits, in fact, had been one reason Tom Foord had opted not to take Kal public. It had made it difficult to reveal fully the performance of the profit-sharing plan to managers and assistant managers for first couple of years of the original plan's existence, Ken notes ruefully. "I'd be standing there each year trying to tell them the results of their plan without telling them what the actual profit was, or their percentage," he laughs. "We did that for a while then screwed up our courage and said if this is going to work we need to make full disclosure of profits and loss."

TEAM SHARE: CHANGING THE NATURE OF WORK

The notion that full financial disclosure would somehow damage Kal turned out again to be a non-starter when Team Share transformed profit sharing into the 50/50 partnership. In fact, taking transparency the final step by posting stores' individual profit and loss statements on stores' staff-room bulletin boards demonstrated Kal's trust in individuals and its commitment to them. In turn, being better informed made employees feel more a part of the company. "Team Share has been a great motivator and a huge educator," says Ken. "It really fosters team-based decisions, and aligns what's best for team members with what's best for the company."

Store managers adjusted as well. In effect, the traditional pyramid-shaped reporting structure, with a broad base rising to a point, had been inverted to create a top-down structure. Managers saw themselves accountable first to customers, then to their people, and then to management at head office. Instead of feeling stuck out in the back pounding on tires all day, service people now had an incentive to understand more about how the business worked.

Perhaps most important of all, Team Share reinforced the fact that a store's profitability increased with productivity — and productivity improved when individuals worked as part of a team. "Being able to track how well they did every month completely changed the nature of their work," says Ken.

Team Share quickly achieved the desired goal of inspiring employees at the operating level to focus on efficiency as the handmaiden of profits. Staff began thinking like owners instead of employees, and paid

Team Share has been a great motivator and a huge educator. It really fosters team-based decisions, and aligns what's best for employees with what's best for the company.

more attention to costs. "People in stores were discussing whether they should replace that tire balancer for $10,000, or repair it for $1,500," Ken says. "And since the guys running the balancer had a good opinion on what might work best, the managers listened to what they had to say. As everybody took on more responsibility, the system created more effective teams."

While the 50/50 partnership achieved Kal's goal of grabbing the attention of employees, its generosity also amazed some of Kal's business peers, and would continue to do so for years. Archie Stroh recalls the topic of pensions coming up during a conversation with the owner of an auto-glass chain. "He said, 'You're going to think I'm crazy, but we're giving our employees 20 percent of the profits,'" says Archie. "I laughed and trumped that. I told him, 'Then you're going to think we're lunatics, because we're giving ours 50 percent.'"

In addition to benefiting present employees, the 50/50 plan assisted in recruiting new ones, Archie says. Even better, he believes it does what the old B Partnership plan failed to do: it appeals to candidates with an entrepreneurial bent who fit into Kal's business model. "If your business is spread out all over the place, like ours is, you need people who can make their own decisions," he says. "We didn't need a guy who makes the same mistakes over and over, or who's like a lemming and blindly follows the crowd over a cliff without considering alternatives. We want people who challenge our thinking. I love guys who bend the rules, trying to find a newer and better way. Profit sharing, which rewards people on the basis of their performance, attracts that kind of person."

MAKING SAFETY A PRIORITY

By 1998 Kal Tire's payroll topped 2,000 employees. Yet it still lacked a human resources department or an occupational health and safety unit. The oversight was partly attributable to Kal's decentralized structure. Tom Foord had always left problems in those areas to store managers to deal with on an ad hoc basis. To Tom's son-in-law Ken Kurbis, though, Kal had become too big to ignore human resources and safety as corporate priorities.

Ken, a lawyer who joined Kal in 1997 as legal counsel, had an affinity for counseling employees that led to founding a fledgling HR department. His continuing advocacy for safer work practices, bolstered by evidence in the form of Workers'

Above: Ken Kurbis.

No

Safety #1
All team me

priority. M...

...bers to Atte...

The programs broadened Kal's capabilities and qualifications. Safety became an awesome selling feature. We started upgrading all sorts of procedures.

Compensation Board claims, had perhaps a greater impact. Archie Stroh, already predisposed to ensuring a best-practices approach was built into all Kal's activities, agreed that safety should be included among them. In 1997, he added safety to the responsibilities of Bruce Walkden, newly hired as Kal's equipment and vehicle manager. Archie left few doubts in Bruce's mind as to the priority Kal was prepared to give to safety. "When I asked what my budget was," Bruce says, "Archie replied, 'What budget? What do you need? Just do it.'"

On his first tour of Kal's stores, Bruce reacted instinctively to safety lapses he identified. In Sparwood, B.C., an earthmover tire had dropped from a forklift and rolled out of a warehouse; he ordered the doors of the building narrowed to contain errant tires, then established a company-wide policy to govern the size of equipment used to move tires. In Nelson, he put an end to the practice of servicemen dropping tires one storey from a second-floor storage area to get them to the service area below.

He also tightened procedures governing service calls. Servicemen who missed a last ferry home, or encountered bad weather while on a call and out of range of mobile phones and radios, occasionally spent the night in their trucks and returned to the shop when able. Bruce initiated a sign-out policy that required servicemen to estimate their time of return; if an employee failed to show up, it became Kal policy to send someone to find him.

Archie made sure Bruce got support from Kal to execute his safety campaign. Servicemen often loaded temperature-sensitive equipment in the cab of their trucks in winter so the equipment would work in the field in freezing conditions. Realizing that tools can become deadly projectiles in the case of an accident, Bruce donned his vehicle-and-equipment manager's hat and had Kal's fleet of service trucks modified to include items such as heated tool boxes, permanently attached compressors, and hydraulic tailgates to assist in handling tires in the field.

Employees, of course, were the target beneficiaries of the new focus on safety. And a drop in both WCB claims and days lost to injury suggested that it was working. But Kal still didn't have an overarching policy governing safety, especially on mining sites. And an incident in Fort McMurray gave Kal a glimpse of the consequences if it didn't develop one.

When Kal acquired Tire Town in 1991, it inherited its service contracts with operators in the oil sands. Flemming Sorensen and George Frame have continued to maintain and renew contracts with companies such as Syncrude, Suncor and Albian Sands. Archie, who oversaw the mining group, often lent support from Vernon. Though not easily shaken, Archie recalls being distinctly uncomfortable after one relatively routine session to discuss a contract bid when a manager from Syncrude casually asked if he could get a copy of Kal's mine-site safety policies and procedures. "We had had an excellent safety record," Archie says, "but mine-site safety policies and procedures? We didn't have anything like that."

Kal managed to cobble together a safety policy document that satisfied the client and averted a loss of business. But the event was a wakeup call. If Kal was going to play in the big leagues — and the billion-dollar tar sands projects qualified — it had to go beyond Bruce Walkden's efficient but reactive approach of eliminating bad safety practices. It had to become proactive in developing a coherent mine-site safety policy that prevented them in the first place.

As a first step, Archie hired experience. Leigh-Ann Stewart, a registered and highly qualified safety professional, came on board to augment the efforts of the overworked Bruce Walkden. She also spearheaded development of an overarching safety policy — with special attention to the mining industry that was accounting for a steadily bigger slice of Kal's business.

The newly empowered safety team identified areas of high risk at mine sites. Then Bruce Cantalope designed and created videos and manuals to demonstrate the safest procedures for dealing with OTR tires in those environments. The safety videos showed tires in the process of "zippering" (blowing up) during inflation, and the dangers of failing to monitor tire pressure, which is a primary cause of sidewall

KAL TIRE
True Service

his Team Has Worked **2676** Days
thout A Lost Time Accider

est Previous Record Was

Days GZ **693**

Help Make A New Record
WORK SAFE

Fernie Martin at Highland Valley Copper. **Opposite:** Safety poster titled "Defuse the Bomb" graphically highlights the ever-present danger of tires "zippering" or blowing up, and explains how to avoid the mishap.

weakening. On-site training sessions accompanied the collateral material to give technicians instruction in operating the type of cranes they'd actually be using to handle tires weighing several tons.

Positive customer response and a measurable reduction in employee downtime due to injury encouraged Kal to become even more ambitious in developing safer procedures and equipment. The company was also pleasantly surprised by an unintended consequence of its heightened safety efforts. Industrial customers with special equipment demands, such as tire-handling in hazardous-materials environments, recognized Kal's willingness to train staff, and gladly offered company-specific programs that met specific needs. The programs broadened Kal's capabilities and qualifications. "Safety became an awesome selling feature," says Bruce Walkden. "We started upgrading all sorts of procedures. Kal Tire trained its guys in hazardous gases, for instance, and once the gas plants caught onto this, we got a lot of business in Western Canada. We were the only tire company qualified."

"After we started working on safety issues, there was a mind-shift," says Leigh-Ann. "People's attitudes changed from an acceptance of injuries as

EXPORTING SAFETY, EXPERIENCE ... AND TRUCKS

By 1999, Bruce Walkden, Kal's equipment and vehicle manager (in addition to working on safety with Leigh-Ann Stewart), customized Kal's trucks with safety-inspired, state-of-the-art materials-handling systems. Kal replaced solid metal platforms with grates so dirt could fall through, and substituted the breakage-prone cab-top "gum-ball machine" lights with brighter, more durable strobes similar to those used by the police.

Behind the cab, vehicles were equipped with portable cages to enclose tires and protect operators against blowouts during inflation after repair or installation. Kal also installed automatic lifts on service trucks to assist workers hoisting tires and equipment on and off trucks, and added swing-down aluminum stairs to give servicemen easier access to truck beds. Instead of investing in new tire-mounting apparatus, Kal rebuilt existing equipment, an environmentally sound practice that also saved money.

By 2008, the vehicles and equipment department had become so proficient at developing specialized systems and technology for tire service in the field that Bruce felt justified in applying for a federal research-and-development grant to fund more innovations. Kal's trucks, once refitted to reduce hazards and to improve ergonomics, were state-of-the-art in the industry, field-tested in Canada, and had helped establish Kal as an industry leader.

Having its equipment pass muster in one of the world's toughest operating environments had another benefit for Kal. In 1996, Ken Finch and Archie Stroh visited Chile to explore the potential for OTR business in the country's growing number of mines. In 1997, the plan took hold when Kal bought a small section-repair plant in Antofagasta, a city in northern Chile that served as a mining industry service centre and shipping port.

The Chilean venture also presented an opportunity to Bruce Walkden. He was able to offset the customized, tire-service trucks' considerable development costs — and even generate a small profit — by exporting vehicles to Chile and Argentina to help Kal service its new mining tire market in those countries.

part of the job, to the understanding that injuries are preventable and unacceptable. If you ever want to see if a company really cares about its team, go have a look at the safety department. If people come to work for us, we're going to make sure they get home safely."

Kal has continued to ensure that safety doesn't slide in importance. Unlike a typical hierarchical structure, Kal's department heads don't typically report to the president. Under Ken Finch, however, Leigh-Ann became the exception at Kal: she reported directly to Ken and continues to report to his successor, Robert Foord. "The policy is more than merely symbolic," Ken says. "It emphasizes the kind of priority we place on workplace safety and the respect we have for our team members."

I hung onto George like you wouldn't believe. He was my tower of strength.

FAREWELL TO GEORGE MILLER

Kal lost one of its most enduring figures — and Tom Foord his dearest friend — when George Miller died on October 15, 1998, at 86. George began his relationship with Kal as a financial consultant in 1959 when he was still with the accounting firm KPMG in Vancouver. He quickly established a personal bond with Tom Foord that lasted the rest of his life. He also became a partner in Kal Tire. Over his association with Kal that lasted nearly 40 years, George participated in virtually every phase of Kal's development — as Tom's trusted wingman and invaluable business resource and as Kal's unrelenting conscience. "I hung onto George like you wouldn't believe," Tom Foord says. "He was my tower of strength."

George's self-confidence emerged early in his career. In 1930, as an 18-year-old, he'd abruptly quit his job with a bank when it refused to promote him to replace a departing senior employee. Upon becoming an accountant, he continued to show complete faith in his own abilities.

George and Tom's personalities complemented one another perfectly. George's business savvy and his readiness to implicitly trust in his own judgment played off of Tom's more courtly approach to business, even if George's aggressive take-no-prisoners style occasionally startled Tom. "Sometimes I wanted to dive under the table when George got going with a company president," Tom laughs. "He wouldn't take any nonsense, and sometimes he could be pretty rough."

George could be just as tough on Kal's employees. His routine visits to Vernon from his Vancouver office, and his singular ability to spot items that he felt needed to be addressed, tended to set everyone at head office walking on eggshells. "George was the hawk," Allan Jewell recalls from his days as Kal's vice-president of purchasing and distribution. "Whenever he came to Vernon I wanted to close my door and hide. I knew he was going to come all the way up the hall to my office and challenge me on every statement and every move I'd ever made."

One of George's greatest contributions, in Ken Finch's view, was his ability to detect any drift from corporate focus and redirect it back to finances, which he considered paramount. George saw diligent attention to financial matters as being in the best interests of employees. "He felt if you didn't pay attention to the financial part of the business you'd wreck the futures of all your team members," Ken says. "When you're in a people business, it's easy to get caught up in trying to do the right thing by people. But in the end, it's the bank that's going to measure whether you're successful or not. George never lost sight of that."

As widely as George was respected at Kal, Ken admits that most felt a palpable relief in Vernon when he departed for Vancouver. "It was 'Phew, George is gone,'" Ken says. "Not that we didn't want to see him again, but man oh man, those sessions were tough. He always asked all the right questions, and when we didn't have answers he'd remind us that maybe we hadn't done all our homework. We swore the next time he came, we'd have the answers."

As significant as George's efforts had been on behalf of Kal — the company whose culture he'd helped shape — Kal sustained him in return. George carried on working on behalf of Kal Tire well into his 80s, long after he'd retired from KPMG. "It energized and exhilarated him," says his widow, Betty. "Tom was a great personal friend, and George's goal was always to help Kal Tire with its success. The dining room table was piled high with papers and folders; we'd eat our meals amidst the organized confusion."

George is remembered in a number of places at Kal, including in photos of him and Tom that have graced both Tom's and Robert Foord's desks. But Ken Finch maintains George's greatest legacy is the ethics that he helped plant and subsequently nurtured at Kal. "When it came to ethics, his view was always, 'Don't cut corners, and never try to hide things. Do the right thing and you'll sleep better at night,'" says Ken. "Those principles are fundamental to the way we've always operated and we owe George a debt of gratitude for engraining them in our culture. He was one of a kind, and a great mentor to Tom and to all of us."

When it came to ethics, his view was always, 'Don't cut corners, and never try to hide things. Do the right thing and you'll sleep better at night.' Those principles are fundamental to the way we've always operated and we owe George a debt of gratitude for engraining them in our culture. He was one of a kind, and a great mentor to Tom and to all of us.

Opposite: George Miller (left), Tom's mentor and closest friend, died October 15, 1998. This photo has graced the desks of both Tom and his son Robert, the current Kal Tire president.

CHAPTER SEVEN: REFINING THE KAL CONCEPT

(THE 2000s)

> ❝ It's knowing how far we go to exceed customers' expectations. ❞

SUCCESSFUL MANAGEMENT SUCCESSION

It was tempting to group and label Kal Tire's 47 years of achievement in terms of time periods, or activities, or management teams as it rolled into the new millennium. But doing so would have ignored Kal's most distinctive characteristic — a singular consistency of focus on progressive improvement.

Kal's management structure contributed immensely to that consistency. In 2000, founder Tom Foord was still the only president Kal had ever had. But he'd showed an uncommon ability to attract supporting casts. George Miller had been at his side for 40 years. Throughout the 1950s and '60s, Jim Lochhead, Colin Campbell and Jack Kristensen were loyal contributors.

When he'd needed more depth, he handpicked new managers, as much for their personal qualities as for their résumés, then carefully slotted them into the organization. During the 1970s, Archie Stroh (1970), Richard Hamilton (1973), Bruce Cantalope (1974), Larry Wynn (1974), Gary Morris (1979) and Robert Kehler (1979) joined Kal. Their staggered arrival ensured smooth succession; all would eventually join Tom Foord as senior-management team members. Also during the 1970s, 1980s and 1990s, Joe Peshko, Flemming Sorensen and George Frame essentially created Kal's mining group.

Amazingly, no senior managers left Kal, except through retirement. In fact, the company's expansion, both organic and through acquisition, had created a seemingly inexorable demand for management talent. To fill it, Kal saw no reason not to carry on its proven practice of hiring the best person available, then allocating the talent where needed.

It worked well when retirements did occur, such as Richard Hamilton's in 1996 and Bruce Cantalope's two years later, as seasoned candidates were waiting in the wings within Kal. When new prospects weren't recognizable or immediately available from within the company, Kal selected from outside the company. Notable hires in the 1980s included Ken Finch (1980), Robert Foord (1987) and Allan Jewell (1988).

The upshot was that Kal entered the new millennium with the strongest management pool it had ever had. The company was as strong as it had ever been. It began 2000 with 160 stores spread from Vancouver to the Ontario border. It had both consolidated the fragmented tire business through acquisitions, and opened its own new outlets set up to its own specifications. With 50 years of experience to call on, Kal set out to maximize the performance of its stores.

Ken Finch succeeded Bruce Cantalope as vice-president of stores in 1998. He and Archie Stroh, Kal's vice-president and general manager, put together a list of outlets that had turned around after being poor performers to become sales leaders. They then assembled a team consisting of senior zone managers Danny Funk, Ed Lauer and Robert Kehler to develop a strategy to apply the successful practices in other Kal locations.

Opposite, clockwise from top left: New Kal Tire stores in 2005, including Kelowna, Port Kells, Edmonton, Grande Prairie and Westbank.

Since Kal now had the capital and confidence to do so, Ken and the store team inaugurated a program of overhauling stores, a process intended to upgrade the chain generally. A component of Ken's plan was to improve the sales and management skills of the store managers. To do so he built on a training syllabus that Bruce Cantalope had developed. Robert Kehler, a senior zone manager who would succeed Ken as vice-president of stores in 2005, recalls executing much of the reconditioning strategy and adding his own competitive message to the managers' education: "We chased our competitors' customers," Robert says. "We chased the business hard, got a bigger market share and built still more stores."

The competitive approach proved as adaptable to downturns as to booms. "When B.C. started going through a period of slow growth, people's mindsets shifted," Robert says. "I looked on it as an opportunity. If a guy in one of our stores told me his business wasn't growing, I pointed out that if he had competitors who had customers, then he had potential new customers. It was as simple as that."

"Amazingly, no senior managers left Kal, except through retirement. In fact, the company's expansion, both organic and through acquisition, had created a seemingly inexorable demand for management talent."

Kal Tire's managment team in 2002 (L-R): Archie Stroh, VP and GM; Allan Jewell, VP Purchasing and Marketing; Tom Foord, President; Bob Wallis, CFO; Robert Foord, VP Sales; Ken Finch, VP Stores and Retread.

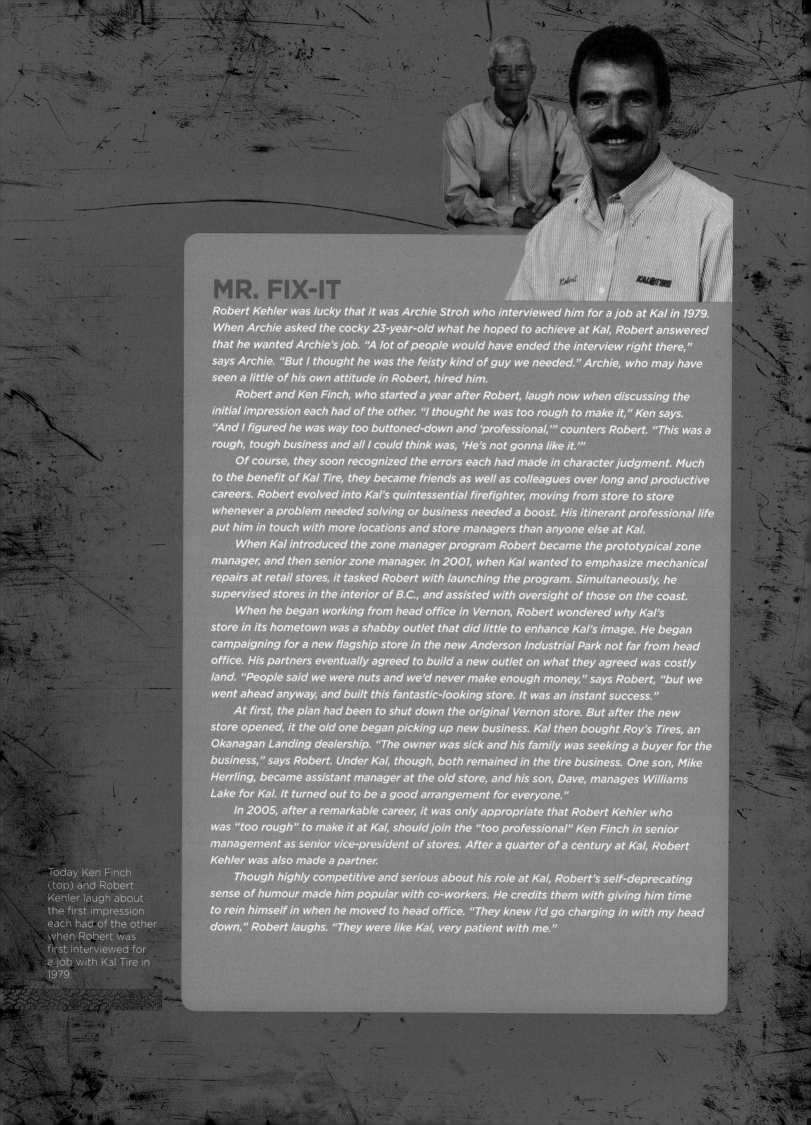

MR. FIX-IT

Robert Kehler was lucky that it was Archie Stroh who interviewed him for a job at Kal in 1979. When Archie asked the cocky 23-year-old what he hoped to achieve at Kal, Robert answered that he wanted Archie's job. "A lot of people would have ended the interview right there," says Archie. "But I thought he was the feisty kind of guy we needed." Archie, who may have seen a little of his own attitude in Robert, hired him.

Robert and Ken Finch, who started a year after Robert, laugh now when discussing the initial impression each had of the other. "I thought he was too rough to make it," Ken says. "And I figured he was way too buttoned-down and 'professional,'" counters Robert. "This was a rough, tough business and all I could think was, 'He's not gonna like it.'"

Of course, they soon recognized the errors each had made in character judgment. Much to the benefit of Kal Tire, they became friends as well as colleagues over long and productive careers. Robert evolved into Kal's quintessential firefighter, moving from store to store whenever a problem needed solving or business needed a boost. His itinerant professional life put him in touch with more locations and store managers than anyone else at Kal.

When Kal introduced the zone manager program Robert became the prototypical zone manager, and then senior zone manager. In 2001, when Kal wanted to emphasize mechanical repairs at retail stores, it tasked Robert with launching the program. Simultaneously, he supervised stores in the interior of B.C., and assisted with oversight of those on the coast.

When he began working from head office in Vernon, Robert wondered why Kal's store in its hometown was a shabby outlet that did little to enhance Kal's image. He began campaigning for a new flagship store in the new Anderson Industrial Park not far from head office. His partners eventually agreed to build a new outlet on what they agreed was costly land. "People said we were nuts and we'd never make enough money," says Robert, "but we went ahead anyway, and built this fantastic-looking store. It was an instant success."

At first, the plan had been to shut down the original Vernon store. But after the new store opened, it the old one began picking up new business. Kal then bought Roy's Tires, an Okanagan Landing dealership. "The owner was sick and his family was seeking a buyer for the business," says Robert. Under Kal, though, both remained in the tire business. One son, Mike Herrling, became assistant manager at the old store, and his son, Dave, manages Williams Lake for Kal. It turned out to be a good arrangement for everyone."

In 2005, after a remarkable career, it was only appropriate that Robert Kehler who was "too rough" to make it at Kal, should join the "too professional" Ken Finch in senior management as senior vice-president of stores. After a quarter of a century at Kal, Robert Kehler was also made a partner.

Though highly competitive and serious about his role at Kal, Robert's self-deprecating sense of humour made him popular with co-workers. He credits them with giving him time to rein himself in when he moved to head office. "They knew I'd go charging in with my head down," Robert laughs. "They were like Kal, very patient with me."

Today Ken Finch (top) and Robert Kehler laugh about the first impression each had of the other when Robert was first interviewed for a job with Kal Tire in 1979.

True Service.

TRUE SERVICE AND THE WOW FACTOR

As Kal found traction, management saw an opportunity to add more mechanical repairs and maintenance to its range of products, building on one of the business areas of its newly acquired outlets. After succeeding Ken Finch as head of stores, Robert Kehler put together a team that spent eight weeks on the road, visiting outlets to verify their potential for more services.

At the same time, Kal overhauled its marketing program. It retired Richard Hamilton's now decade-old marketing campaign that centred on the theme of "Good, Better, Best" and the slogan "If we sell it, we guarantee it" that Tom Foord had been delivering in TV commercials. In its place it launched a new campaign based on the catchphrase "True Service" that was felt to better represent the shift into retail and mechanical services. When the campaign was launched in the spring of 2004, the operative word "WOW" was added. The objective of the campaign was to emphasize "service beyond expectations" that left customers with a sense of WOW.

Another strategy focused on customer referrals, already a source of growth for Kal. Business cards with a sticker on the back urged satisfied customers to tell five friends about their experience. The simple-sounding campaign (which would be later be called viral marketing) exceeded expectations. Kal was suddenly flooded with letters, phone calls and e-mail. "It became our new marketing secret," says Robert Kehler.

The objective of the campaign was to emphasize "service beyond expectations" that left customers with a sense of WOW.

FROM GOLD MINES TO THE GOLDEN HORSESHOE: EXPANDING INTO ONTARIO

As Kal's bright orange and blue colours became more widely recognized in the West, its determined effort to deliver Kal-branded service that was, as its ads claimed, "beyond expectations" continued to attract customers. Strengthening the brand, moreover, had helped it successfully absorb newly acquired outlets into the Kal family. With those successes Kal began casting a corporate eye east toward Ontario, the biggest market in Canada.

Aware that it was breaking new ground, Kal hoped to become comfortable by first moving into northern Ontario towns and cities with resource-based economies similar to those around many of its western locations. In 2000, it purchased The Tire People, a five-outlet business based in Sudbury, from its owner-operators, Guy Desjardins, John Mathewman, Jim Martin and Jim Stewart. The company consisted of a Bandag retread plant, two retail stores, a commercial centre and an OTR shop. It had branches in New Liskeard, Sault St. Marie, Kirkland Lake and North Bay. It also had one in Rouyn-Noranda, a small Quebec copper-mining city close to the Ontario border.

Later in 2000, Kal added Timmins Tire to strengthen its northern Ontario presence. In both cases, Kal followed its usual practice of leaving existing management in place. The thinking was that the managers knew their markets and by leveraging that with Kal's resources could improve their outlets' performances.

The initial plan had been to solidify the northern Ontario businesses under the Kal banner, then use the new outlets as a springboard from which to move south. In 2002, Kal finally edged into Canada's richest market, the Golden Horseshoe along the north shore of Lake Ontario. It partnered with J&M Tire, an OTR business based in Oshawa that had branches in Hamilton and Mississauga. Shortly thereafter, Kal acquired Central Tire in London, in western Ontario.

Kal's growth over the years had always appeared outwardly smooth. Acquisition experience helped it spot potential problem areas in time to avoid them or minimize their impact until they could be rectified. Even so, some aspects of expansion remained bothersome. The quest for good managers, for example, was virtually perpetual, and it took on a new urgency when new outlets were opened or purchased.

But chief among Kal's expansion challenges was finding a way to spread its culture across a network of stores that were spread farther and farther from Vernon. And failure to come up with a reliable method was not for lack of trying. Indeed, Kal had enjoyed considerable success in training existing or new managers of acquired stores. In addition to providing guidance and supervision, zone managers and senior zone managers were expected to inculcate Kal's culture in the staff of stores they oversaw. But while the company tried to maintain its custom of having at least one senior manager visit each store annually, growth made it all but impossible for the six-man senior management team to find the time as the store count passed 200.

To some extent the move into Ontario exacerbated the problem: it was farther than ever from head office, had characteristics different from other markets Kal was in, and overextended Kal's human resources. "Management a couple of thousand miles away in Vernon was certainly aware of the challenges created by the cost of expansion — financially and in terms of time and human resources," says Ken Finch. "But we also knew we had to be in Ontario and had seized a good opportunity to enter the market. Experience in the West gave us confidence that our taking a long-term approach would work in the end." Nonetheless, Kal recognized that the reward it saw down the road carried heightened risk. "A single mistake that used to cost $5,000 in the old days now cost much more in Ontario," Ken says.

SPEED BUMPS ON THE HIGHWAY EAST

Imprinting Kal Tire's culture was a challenge at the best of times; without a strong Kal Tire presence in the stores, it became impossible. What had begun in a flourish of opportunity was looking worrisome from Vernon, Ken Finch acknowledges. "If we couldn't spread our culture we couldn't expand our business," he says.

Kal was already well along in executing its Ontario expansion when it recognized that its strategy was at risk of going off the rails. Rather than buy the Ontario companies outright, Kal had become a shareholder in them. The plan had been to leave existing managers — now Kal's partners in the businesses — in place, run the stores independently, and then buy the remaining shares and turn them into Kal outlets when it had enough people to run them.

The strategy was supposed to address the need to act promptly on opportunities when they arose, despite a shortage of managers, says Bob Wallis, who succeeded Larry Wynn in 2001 as Kal's chief financial officer. "We knew we didn't have the people to send down and manage the stores, but to stake a claim in Ontario we had to become shareholders in these businesses when they were available."

The timing of the move into Ontario, however, wasn't propitious. By 2002, as Kal was tidying up the London transaction, Ontario's service- and manufacturing-based economy (as opposed to resource-based in the West) began to crater. In turn, the economic downdraft threatened to suck Kal's Ontario strategy down with it. "The people who ran those stores kept turning to us for direction, and we tended to start meddling," says Bob Wallis. "It confused the lines of authority and responsibility, and nobody knew who was in charge."

Along with the strain on operations, Ken Finch says the situation compromised Kal's ability to establish its core values which he believed sacrosanct. "To make the AIMS work, they had to be thoroughly understood and lived by on a daily basis."

Ken can easily list the Kal qualities that he believes define a Kal employee — which he felt were lacking in the Ontario stores: "It's knowing that you wear a clean uniform and shave every morning. It's insisting that the people who change tires also greet customers and sell tires. It's going through rigorous training, which teaches the servicemen to be businessmen. It's knowing how far we go to exceed customers' expectations."

As though those shortfalls weren't enough of an impediment to the integration of Kal's new partners, the acquired companies also tended to believe that profits alone drove the business — a contradiction to Kal. Part of the problem was that Kal had failed to accurately communicate its operating style, Ken concedes. It had simply assumed that the new outlets would recognize that had profitability been its primary business motive, Kal would have stayed in the West where it could be the price leader by virtue of its high market share.

It's insisting that the people who change tires also greet customers and sell tires. It's going through rigorous training, which teaches the servicemen to be businessmen.

Opposite: Invoices carrying Kal Tire's true service promise wait for customers in a store's sales and service centre.

Ontario was not without its bright spots. Smaller cities and towns in the north, for instance, were similar to those in Kal's heartland in the West — resource-based centres where Kal had a mix of commercial and retail business and understood its markets. In the south, by contrast, Kal encountered a less familiar economy. Trucking fleets were huge, with high-volume tire needs that generated low gross margins. They were accustomed to buying tires directly from manufacturers, leaving dealers with only a distribution commission and an installation fee — not Kal Tire's preferred way of doing business.

What was more, competitors in the new market hadn't historically emphasized service, Kal's strength. Instead the eastern market had evolved into one based solely on price, which meant Kal's Ontario stores would need to generate far greater volume than those out west typically did.

LEARNING TO SERVE A NEW TYPE OF CUSTOMER

Unused to failure, Kal was rattled by its inability to roll unimpeded into Canada's biggest province. In its haste to seize a perceived opportunity, it had not sufficiently analyzed its new business environment. In retrospect, Archie Stroh believes Kal was serving a different breed of customer in Ontario using the same methods that had worked for 50 years in the West. "We tried to Kal Tire-ize the stores before we really understood the needs of our customers," he says. "These big self-sustaining commercial customers required a completely different level of service and communication. Customers who have one or two trucks come to our stores for their needs. But in Ontario, customers were too big to visit us; you had to go to their yard, they didn't come to yours."

Determined to turn its operations around in Ontario, Kal resorted to its characteristic grittiness to adapt to the realities of the Ontario market. Its business was built on the belief that superior service can command a premium price. Adapting to an Ontario market that viewed tires as a commodity that traded solely on price was tough for Kal to do without compromising its time-honoured business model, Ken Finch notes.

So Kal decided to continue to extol service as its value proposition. "We still felt large customers would eventually start to appreciate the values we offered beyond just the price of tires," Ken says. In fact, five years after it first moved into Ontario, Kal was sufficiently confident that its message was taking hold. The company had come to understand the eastern market — so much so that it decided to grab another opportunity that seemed too good to let slip by. In 2005, it bought Mississauga Tire from Joe Segato, a well-known industry figure.

The Mississauga Tire deal had all the appearances of yet another case of Kal's reach exceeding its grasp. But Ken Finch argues that the deal represented the financial prudence that enabled Kal to seize an opportunity that fit with its long-term strategy, even if it seemed out of sync in the short term. "Joe and his partners were interested in selling, and we approached it as a one-time opportunity," he says. "We had no Kal Tire people in Ontario to run it, or to start putting our processes and culture in place, and although it was premature, the chance to get critical mass quickly was too good a deal to pass up. Remember we think long term."

As part of the deal, Joe Segato remained with Kal to oversee the transformation of Mississauga Tire into Kal, and to help manage Kal's resulting outlets in Ontario. Kal also sent Danny Funk, senior zone manager in Grande Prairie, to Toronto to set up an office and to establish a closer connection between Vernon and Ontario. Joe Segato proved a valuable asset in his own right, remaining on board as a partner in Kal Ontario, putting his experience to use assisting in the administration of what would be 25 Ontario stores by 2009.

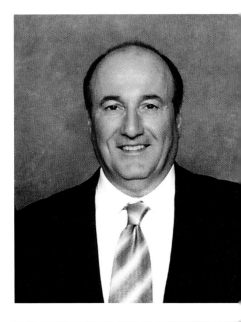

Joe and his partners were interested in selling, and we approached it as a one-time opportunity.

Above: Kal Tire bought Mississauga Tire from Joe Segato in 2005, giving the company a beachhead in the large and very competitive Ontario market.

163

"We still felt large customers would eventually start to appreciate the values we offered beyond just the price of tires."

Most importantly, Kal had penetrated the Ontario market on its own terms. Rather than edge into the province, it had seized opportunities when they arose. Taking a page from Tom Foord's handbook, when he was building the company, management had acted on collective instinct and made a long-term commitment to work out the details.

True, it hadn't always been as prepared as it might have been; problems had ranged from culture clashes and unfamiliar markets to dampened economic conditions and management shortages. For all that, Kal had few regrets. It had landed lucrative stores in key locations throughout Canada's most populous province. Unbound by any need to generate short-term gains, Kal could stick to its long-term vision and fill the gaps between the dots representing existing stores on the map of Ontario, then use its culture to bind them into a cohesive force joined to its operations in the West.

A NEW TEAM
FLEXES ITS MUSCLE

Inevitably time and retirement visited the other parts of the management team who had guided Kal into and through the 1990s. From the middle of the decade to the middle of the next, Kal faced the daunting task of replacing six key executives. Between 1996 and 2000, Richard Hamilton, Gary Morris, Bruce Cantalope and Larry Wynn departed, taking with them a total of 91 years of experience at Kal. The retirement of Archie Stroh in 2005 and Allan Jewell in 2007 cost Kal another 55 years.

Kal's combination of an experienced executive pool and effective recruiting of newcomers smoothed the transition. Robert Kehler already had 26 years of experience at Kal when he took over as vice-president of stores in 2005, replacing Ken Finch — who'd held the job for seven years. Robert Foord was a 10-year Kal veteran when he replaced Gary Morris in 1997. By the time Robert took over responsibility for the mining division from Archie in 2005, he was still only 47, yet had 18 years of experience in Kal's operations.

But Kal discovered that its culture attracted executive talent from outside the company, too. Mark Batchelor, an MBA who worked for Michelin in the U.S. and France, first knew Kal as his biggest customer. In the four years he dealt with Kal, he had been impressed with Kal's unwavering integrity. "We rarely had a meeting where the AIMS weren't incorporated into the decision-making process," Mark says. "Kal had a pretty intimidating presence because of its size, but everybody was so willing to work with us and placed such an emphasis on communication that we were able to resolve the most challenging subjects." That impression, he says, made it easy to accept Kal's offer in 2003 to join Kal.

Allan Jewell's announcement in 2005 that he was looking to retire in a couple of years was both a dilemma and an opportunity for Kal. For the 17 years Allan had spent at Kal, the company had granted his initial wish that he not be involved in strictly accounting matters. Instead, he'd taken over purchasing and marketing, then grafted warehousing and transportation on to those initial responsibilities. All of which created the challenge for Kal when Allan announced his pending retirement: it wasn't going to be easy to find a replacement with Allan's breadth of skills.

Kal found the ideal candidate in John Mullin, a University of Alberta business graduate whose management experience included oversight for branches, warehouses and a transportation network while he was vice-president of operations for Huttig Building Products, a St. Louis, Missouri, building materials company. John subsequently took the position of chief operating officer of the DoALL Company, a privately owned industrial equipment manufacturer headquartered in Wheeling, Illinois, near Chicago. An ownership dispute had developed among the heirs of the founder. DoALL's banks, worried that an ensuing financial slide at the company would impair their investment, pressed the company to hire John to execute a turnaround. "It was an interesting business challenge," John says, "but not a good situation in the long run."

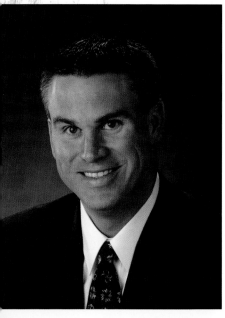

Kal had a pretty intimidating presence because of its size, but everybody was so willing to work with us and placed such an emphasis on communication that we were able to resolve the most challenging subjects.

Kal Tire's pitch appealed to John on a number of levels. Kal had resolved the inter-generational ownership issues he had faced in Chicago. Robert and Colin Foord, along with Ken Finch, were the second generation of the Foord family at Kal. Ken Chaun and Gerald Olstad, respectively sons-in-law of Ken Finch and Colin Foord, were from the third generation of the family. But Kal didn't consider itself a "family-run company" so much as a company that employed relatives of its founder. "It's very unusual for a family-owned business to be set up in a way that it will survive from generation to generation," John says.

The efficiency of store managers operating autonomously, but according to Kal Tire standards, worked for John as well. "Kal makes decisions that can be applied to the entire company," he says. "That means it can grow without having to build a huge central infrastructure. Even if it doubles in size, it still won't require a lot of central controls."

John admits to tripping initially over a couple of Kal's concepts. "I'd worked in businesses that had profit sharing, but maybe 15 percent, never 50," he says, echoing the impression of many upon hearing of the generosity of Kal's 50/50 partnership. He also felt the AIMS lacked the pithiness of a good mission statement. "I thought it was too long and nobody would remember it," he laughs. "But I came to see it as a living document. The AIMS actually affects how Kal Tire conducts itself and represents the values of the company."

In fact, it was one of those values — sincerity, descended from Kal's Canadian small-town roots — that was the clincher. "I was pleased that my children would be raised in Vernon and that I would stay here until I retired," he says.

That Mark and John were the first partners and senior managers Kal hired from outside the company since Robert Foord joined in 1987 and Allan Jewell in 1988 had a certain consistency: Mark was replacing Robert, facilitating his move to head of Kal's mining-tire group; and John Mullin replaced Allan Jewell, two years before Allan was due to retire.

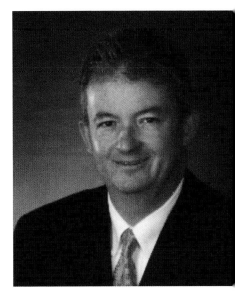

PLANNING FOR A NEW GENERATION

Kal's senior managers had no trouble discussing company matters openly with one another. Yet the topic of Tom Foord's succession plan seldom rose to the top of Kal's meeting agenda. One reason was a natural reluctance of the team to suggest to Tom that the issue was urgent. Although he was 78 in 2000, and controlled Kal financially, urgently insisting that Kal prepare for continuance after he was gone would have suggested that his departure was imminent — which it wasn't.

Nor was Kal likely to be rudderless if Tom did leave suddenly. Either Archie Stroh, the garrulous, can-do face of Kal for 29 years, or Ken Finch, its measured strategist for 19 years, was more than capable of taking over. In fact, Archie and Ken had agreed between them that it made sense that one of them would succeed Tom as president, and that the timing of Tom's decision would determine who it would be. "I'm three years older than Ken," says Archie. "So if Tom decided to give up the presidency earlier, we agreed that I would take over. If he waited longer, it made more sense for Ken to take the job."

In the meantime, they reassured Tom that there was no rush to choose his successor — which Tom admits prolonged his succession decision. A self-confessed procrastinator, he took them at their word. "I couldn't make up my mind what I was going to do," he says, "so I did nothing." When Tom still hadn't decided by 2004, however, Archie, then 62, believed it no longer made sense for him to stay in the running if he'd only be holding the presidency for a couple of years. Instead, he told Tom and Ken that he would be retiring in 2005, after 35 years at Kal.

As was customary Archie, never comfortable with inaction, "got things going" with his decision. Shortly afterward Tom finally announced that he too would retire in June after 51 years as president. "When somebody of Archie's stature announced his intention to retire," he told Kal's assembled managers, sales people and associates, "it gave me cause to seriously reflect on my own role and the future of Kal Tire."

In Kal's new structure, Ken Finch became president. Tom became chairman of Kal's newly created six-man advisory board. Archie, too, was appointed to the board, which included Larry Bell, former chairman of B.C. Hydro and deputy finance minister for the B.C. government; Ross Smith, former managing partner of the accounting firm KPMG; and Phil Wick, former president and CEO of Les Schwab Tire Centers in Oregon.

Archie admits to twinges of retirement remorse since leaving the company he'd helped define — and the job that defined him. Board activities and other projects he undertakes on Kal's behalf have helped him make the transition. So has his winter home in Palm Springs, California, near that of Tom and Norah Foord, which gives him a chance to stay in touch with them.

Nostalgically recalling his career, Archie views it through the lens of his relationship with Tom. The contradictions in their personalities seemed to strengthen the bond between them. "We were an exceptional team, and I love him to bits," Archie says. "He was the long-term thinker and planner and I was the bull in the china shop, charging forward and shaking something, anything, out of the trees to get it going."

Tom, he says, was typically readier to roll the dice on deals than he was, yet not nearly as aggressive as Archie in selling an idea to someone. "Tom was always a really nice, down-to-earth guy who would visit with everybody at the big suppliers," Archie says. "I'd tell him he had to stop talking to everybody and stick to the presidents. Eventually he did that, to our great advantage, but he was always just as content gabbing with the guys in the back shop."

Those personality traits, of course, were among the qualities that made Tom a revered figure at Kal, as well as one of the most respected entrepreneurs in Western Canada. In 2005 he was elected to the Western Canada Tire Dealers Association Hall of Fame. Archie, too, received his due as a tire industry builder and leader. In 2009 he was inducted into the industry hall of fame, where he appropriately shares yet another bond with Tom Foord.

CERTIFYING EXCELLENCE

In the early 1990s, Kal adopted a policy of posting available jobs internally. The objective was to make opportunities available first to its employees — who, after all, already had an affinity for the company. But selecting the right candidate from applicants wasn't always easy. And while there was no evidence of favouritism, there was potential for abuse.

By the middle of the decade, Kal had developed a formal certification system that resolved the issue of a candidate's qualification for a job. The system has evolved since into arguably the most important component of Kal's integrated human resources strategy, a structured process that has elevated certification into one of Kal's highest honours.

Candidates must be certified at the appropriate level to apply for a posted job. Employees work through their supervisors to enter the certification process, which includes Kal-based training programs. Once an employee with sufficient experience has completed the necessary training and shown a comprehensive grasp of Kal's cultural and business principles, he can apply through his supervisor to appear before a certification committee. The committee, consisting of four to six zone managers and senior zone managers, makes the final decision on a candidate's certification.

We wanted certification to become a milestone in a career at Kal, to be certified for an assistant manager's or manager's position. And it has.

Two Work Order System
Counter Person
Sales & Service Technician
Print 2 W/O
#2 on clipboard
for tracking
Complete inspection
on #1 W/O
Switch W/O
#2 goes to technician
Switch W/O
Make quote
Based on inspection
Begin work on vehicle
on #2 W/O
Use new #2 W/O to continue work
Complete work and perform operation no option
Park vehicle
KAL TIRE
True Service
you need.
• Your first aid attendant
are essential should you req
further medical care.
• If you are hurt at work, see your first aid attendant, first. Let us take care of you.
KAL TIRE
True Service.
LABOUR
PASSENGER • LIGHT TRUCK
Passenger Rotate
Ultra Performance Rotate
Passenger Changeover
Passenger Tire Repair
Custom Wheel Changeover

Kal makes no apologies for the fact that the process is grueling for candidates. In fact, it deliberately set the bar high. "Typically, the certification takes three to six hours or so of intensive interviews," Ken Finch says. "People have to be recommended, then work hard to prepare and to show themselves capable in a range of areas. We wanted assistant manager or manager certifications to be a milestone in a career at Kal Tire. And it has."

As the certification process has evolved, it has earned its place in the Kal culture. Ken estimates that only about two-thirds of certification candidates are successful. Those who don't make the cut are given time and advice on what to work on to make their next bid for certification successful. "We want to be constructive," Ken notes. "We certainly don't want to lose those people if we can help it."

The certification program, in concert with a similar, committee-based selection process for choosing from among certified applicants for job openings, has clarified the career paths open to employees. It has also dovetailed with the development of Kal's training modules. In addition to assisting employees to develop skills and confidence, the curriculum feeds into the certification process. That jobs are open only through the internal promotion process and only to certified candidates ensures that the in-house education is relevant and that the promotion process is transparent

The training modules themselves were carefully drawn to focus on skills required for specific positions. At the same time, they demonstrate to participants Kal's willingness to invest in its employees' futures. One of the most gratifying moments, Ken adds, is seeing the process pay off. "One day you see them confidently stand up in front of a group of people they now supervise, and know that they are making a difference," he says. "People find out that they are stronger than they thought, and they just get better and better."

OVERHAULING HUMAN RESOURCES

Kal's long-time practice of assigning new executives to a store for a month or so was initially intended to expose them to the fundamentals of the company's business. Ken Finch cites his stint changing tires and making service calls out of Kal's Lumby store as evidence of the internships' effectiveness. The trenches of tiredom, he says, gave him an appreciation for how hard Kal's front-line people work.

In a roundabout way, the experience also helped inspire Kal's employee benefits programs. In the mid-1980s, Ken's engineer's facility for translating abstract concepts into actual results helped develop AIMS to establish and maintain Kal's values, the 50/50 partnership to fund team members' retirement, and Team Share to give store employees a share of their own outlets' profits.

But while those programs met employees' needs financially, they did little to encourage workers to think of what they did as anything more than a job. In seeking to do that, Ken this time translated the concrete — the actual job of, say, changing tires or selling products — into a more abstract concept — the job as a component in a lifelong career. "I knew if we were doing business properly, the outcome would be customer trust that resulted in more business," he says. "It struck me that from an employee's point of view, if we were doing the right thing, his job would be viewed as the best career possible."

In 2003 Kal labeled the manifestation of that vision as Best Careers. "Our objective was to create an environment where people go home at night feeling fulfilled and satisfied that they've accomplished something, and when they get up in the morning they want to come in to work," Ken says.

Aware that developing customer trust had generated repeat business, Kal Tire saw practical merit in encouraging employees to rethink their employment as a career rather than a job. High employee turnover, particularly among first-year workers, had been bothersome. Reducing it would trim recruiting and training costs, and also build a more experienced workforce. As well, Ken recognized that businesses perform better when employees have a high level of job satisfaction. So Kal would benefit.

To accommodate and promote the concept of Best Careers, Kal began revamping its human resources department. Gary Muuren, promoted from assistant to manager of human resources in 2005, was a proponent of research and began looking into reasons for Kal's high turnover rate, the first step toward finding ways to fix the problem.

Exit interviews with departing employees suggested a trend toward shared domestic and family responsibilities between spouses; employees were less inclined to put in the long hours than they had when a single breadwinner was the family norm. Gary concluded that Kal had to accommodate changing family dynamics and social patterns. "We were finding that the old saying 'Nine to five just won't suffice' needed to be revisited," he says.

Kal also found ways to handle personnel difficulties created by economic disruption. Alberta's booming oil sands projects, for example, were a paradox; although a source of profitable growth for Kal's mining division, the high wages they paid distorted the labour market, attracting workers and making it difficult for Kal to hire staff at its Calgary retread plant. Even if Kal had found workers who hadn't fled to Fort McMurray, it couldn't match oil-patch wages and remain competitive.

Kal's answer typified its new, innovative human resources approach: it created a program in concert with the provincial government to import workers from Mexico. After two years, the workers could return to Mexico for four months, then reapply to enter Canada. If they returned to Kal, they would be allowed to remain in Canada. "The program not only helped stabilize turnover at the Calgary retread plant," says Gary Muuren, "but the plant's performance improved." The result prompted Kal to add 15 Mexican employees to its Edmonton warehouse and seven more in Calgary.

Opposite: Being accepted by Kal Tire's certification process means successful candidates learn everything they need to know about tires. **Above, from top:** As part of its Best Careers program, all new employees attend the Tom Foord Training Center. In 2005 Gary Muuren, who became manager of human resources, was tasked to bring Kal's employment practices in line with changing family dynamics and social patterns in the Canadian workforce.

In keeping with its pragmatic roots, Kal has been careful to incorporate a healthy dose of reality into its human resources program. Experience had proved, for instance, that not everyone is perfectly suited to the job he or she is hired to do. "If that appears to be the case, we ask what we can do to make it so," Ken says. "We suggest it's also the team member's responsibility to talk to the store manager and say, 'There's something here I don't like.'

"But if there's nothing we can do, we also suggest maybe they'd be happier somewhere else," he adds. "It's awfully easy to say nothing, and then for the next 25 years have somebody who's unhappy with his job working at 75 percent capacity."

Kal's training program, championed by Robert Kehler, has played a role in the company's human resources mix. Its scope has broadened to encompass more than 200 training modules that help employees identify and advance along a realistic career path. Training takes place both online and in-person. Courses range from basic safety to management training. Though primarily administered by training specialists in computer-equipped classrooms near the Vernon head office, the program is flexible enough that it can be adapted for delivery elsewhere when required. In 2007, Kal took the curriculum to another level by delivering an automotive apprenticeship program in partnership with Okanagan College.

By refining and adjusting programs as required, Kal had been able to maintain their quality — and as a result, the quality of graduates. Employees seeking to become assistant managers take courses, both online and at the Archie Stroh Training Centre in Vernon, up the street from head office. The practical curriculum includes topics as diverse as AIMS and profit-and-loss statements, required knowledge for those seeking certification.

Ken Finch, who, like all senior management, delivers some aspect of the course to each class, makes no apologies for the difficulty of the certification process. "The committee people will remember the last guy who was 100 percent ready," he says. "The following guys must be up there on the same level. Our standards are much higher than 10 years ago. By 2008, when we were up to 200 stores, we were certifying 40 to 50 people in a year."

For Ken, the Best Careers program and the Kal-ready confidence of its participants have proved personally rewarding. In a sense, the concepts embedded in Best Careers are a reaffirmation of the Kal values that Ken first encountered in the shop of the Lumby store, and which have played a role in his career ever since. "This is the higher purpose of business," he enthuses. "I love that stuff. I love it, because it helped me develop to my potential.

"When I started, I was terrified to get up in front of more than three people. The annual meetings forced me to speak in front of big crowds, and 28 years later I do it very comfortably. Overcoming our fears and weaknesses gives us a lot more self-confidence, and I think we do a pretty good job of challenging people as we move them along."

RATIONALIZING RETAIL

Even as internal systems were being put in place to develop and monitor human resources, the Kal management team, bolstered by enthusiastic newcomers and now presided over by Ken Finch, had started executing its three-pronged strategy — to develop its rapidly growing mining-tire business outside Canada, to carry on the integration of its newly acquired operations in Ontario, and to extend and strengthen the retail side of its business across the country.

Mark Batchelor, Kal's vice-president of sales, grew the sales support team from three to 15 and emphasized service offerings. Programs focused on, among other things, monitoring tire use to save commercial customers money. "We track their mileage and fleet programs, measure all the tread depths and air pressures, and enable our customers to recognize which vehicles need service and at what intervals," Mark says. "We can show, line by line, how much money a customer spends on valve stems, or retreading or after-hours service calls."

Mark took advantage of Kal's human resources initiatives to select and train staff in order to add discipline to its sales force. "The sales team goes to our training school for a week, spends three months in a store for practical experience, and returns to the school for another week," he says. "And we encourage them to mentor others in the store."

John Mullin, meanwhile, had the advantage of having Allan Jewell as his mentor. John acquainted himself with Kal's warehousing and transportation responsibilities while Allan carried on as head of purchasing and marketing. The following year, they switched roles to complete the transition. John found the process effective: "It gave me the chance to understand the history of what had transpired to get us to this point, and it really helped me to understand our history with suppliers."

Tom Foord's occasional presence at John's meetings with suppliers proved an invaluable resource. "He tries not to say anything," says John. "But when he does speak up, the suppliers listen. He's always right on target, and adds a relevant historical perspective. Whatever situation we face today, he has been in a similar position before."

Opposite: As part of Kal Tire's new human resources strategy, the company created a jobs program with Alberta that invited Mexican workers to Canada — the team of workers that Kal imported included (L-R): Jesus Peralta, Ramon "Max" Sanchez, Norton Fast, Juan Marroquin, Fabian Solis, Rodolfo "Rudy" Villaobos, 2007. **Above:** Under Ken Finch's leadership, Kal Tire launched a program to modernize and strengthen the company's retail presence across the country.

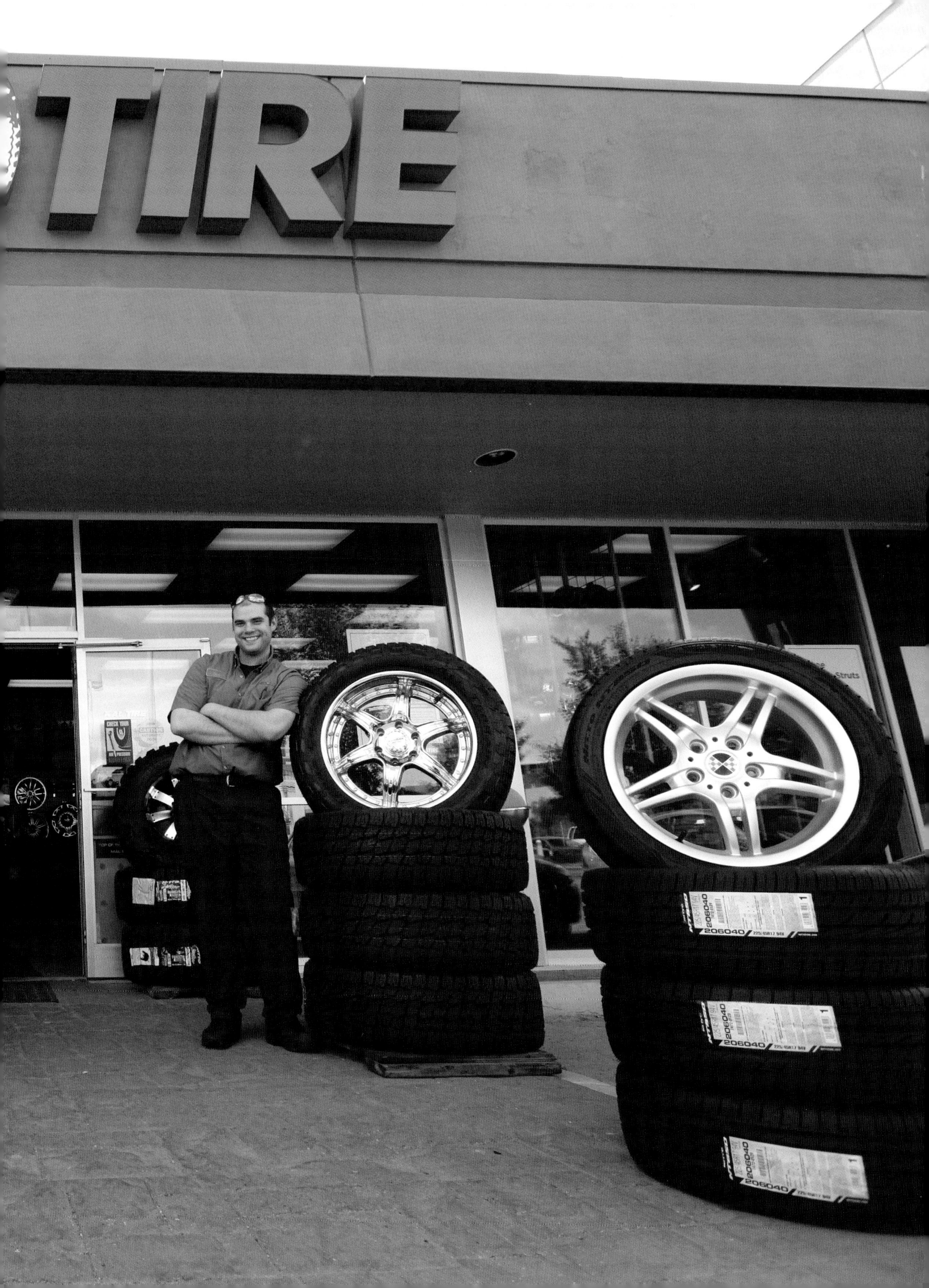
TIRE

A DAY
IN THE LIFE
OF A KAL STORE

Kal Tire's retail operations are often called the lifeblood of the company. Each outlet is alive with activity and customer service, from early morning until closing time. Here, Ed Lauer, who managed a number of outlets before becoming director of stores for Western Canada , gives a quick rundown of a typical day at any one of Kal Tire's large mixed stores.

Early on a winter morning, you'll see headlights coming into the lot with people arriving for work. They'll converge, and then head off in different directions to get the store ready for another day.

> When you've given the customer great service and they say WOW, then we've met AIM Number One: to exceed the customer's expectations.
>
> — Ed

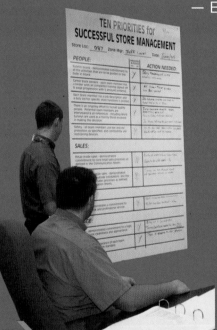

FIRST THINGS FIRST
Some team members are prepping for meetings, some are clearing snow from the front, others are checking in with the senior dispatcher and someone starts making coffee.

BEFORE THE DOORS OPEN
Several people are gathering for a management meeting to exchange thoughts on how to improve service, go over results of the previous week and set goals for the coming week. Also on the agenda: career tracking and setting up mentoring programs and appraisals. But at the top of the list is the big question: How often are customers experiencing the WOW factor?

Service people are checking in with senior dispatch for the day's calls, so they can get to their fleets first thing. Team members are sending out trucks, double checking and moving inventory around so they have the right tires ready for today's jobs. Someone turns on the popcorn machine for the customers.

"We don't over-complicate things, and we always go back to the basics, which bring value to the customer and create successful and consistent results. Often it just means being interested and understanding their business and personal needs. "

Administrative people are starting to arrive to check the previous day's results and prepare cash reports, for review by the general manager and assistant manager. The service trucks are already on the road. Customers are being greeted.

A sales meeting (with as many as three to ten salespeople, depending on the store) covers what's happening in the marketplace, competitive issues to deal with, special deals for customers, getting more customers in for mechanical services and, always, WOWing the customer. Emphasis is placed on ways to collect customer information so the store can deliver great service. Outside, a transport truck is unloading product. Customers are waiting at the door.

OUR DAY BEGINS *Kal Tire technicians are on the truck pad fixing flats or replacing tires on vehicles. Product is rolling in from the retread plant. Phones are ringing and salespeople are busily calling customers. Many customers are already there, deep in conversation with the salespeople behind the service podiums. As they say, the joint is jumping.*

"Picture this," says Ed. "Each outlet has a showroom set up with service podiums ready to help customers. These open areas are filled with tire racks, new wheels and other shiny new products."

The TV is on, customers are watching the news or reading magazines, children are playing with video games in the corner, a couple of guys sit on stools watching their vehicles being worked on, the coffee's percolating and you can hear popcorn popping in the back. The whole place smells of popcorn and tires. The phones are ringing and everywhere, Kal Tire staff are welcoming people. It's a busy, humming, high energy atmosphere, with team members showing a sense of urgency, running to the customer, sharing information, providing quality service, earning the customers' trust and knowing that working in the store is their best career.

" Customers sense that we want to take care of them. When you walk in, the energy is palpable. That's the way it is when a store is right. "

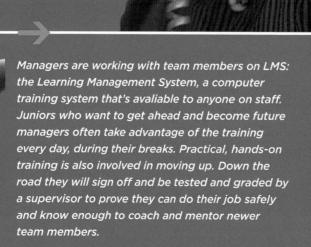

Managers are working with team members on LMS: the Learning Management System, a computer training system that's available to anyone on staff. Juniors who want to get ahead and become future managers often take advantage of the training every day, during their breaks. Practical, hands-on training is also involved in moving up. Down the road they will sign off and be tested and graded by a supervisor to prove they can do their job safely and know enough to coach and mentor newer team members.

LUNCH TIME: IN FULL SWING *Kal Tire team members usually take a half-hour lunch. Most people stay in, and go to the lunch room where people come and go throughout the break.*

> # When people ask how late we're open, the answer should be until the last customer leaves.

MID-AFTERNOON: IT'S HUMMING *The store has a mix of commercial and retail services, so it's always full of customers. Some look on as work is being done on their vehicle, while others are being educated on any number of subjects, from retreads vs. new tires, to mileage tracking. Retreads are always an option for medium-size trucks, promoting reduced cost per mile and a greener environment. One customer is reviewing a scrap tire report with his salesman, to determine possible causes of casing failure.*

Out in the shop, doors are opening and closing all the time, vehicles are driven in and guided onto hoists. Work orders are flowing constantly. Team members are doing tire rotations and kibitzing with their customers. They look like they're having fun, even while discussing more serious matters like correct air pressure.

> ## It really is something exciting to watch when it's working well.

Sales staff are still calling on customers. From the latest updates, they know which products their customers have purchased, and which ones could work even better for them.

The place is abuzz with activity. Customers are coming in from their trucks and are jumping in to help change tires.

GETTING LATE: NO SIGN OF SLOWING DOWN
For some customers, the circle is complete. Team members have greeted them at the front door, the service people have given them a running commentary on the work they're doing and now they are being presented with their vehicle, with thanks for their business. They have had a WOW experience and will tell their friends.

By 7:00 p.m. most stores have locked their doors, but many outlets aren't done yet. There might be a customer with a special need that a team member is helping to solve. Kal employees stick with it until they are happy.

"On any day after a first snowfall, stores can be open as late as 10 o'clock," says Ed.

Guys start washing down the floor and emptying garbage pails. The ones who could have gone home an hour ago are still standing around talking, some of them lingering in the comfortable customer waiting area, comparing how many tires they've sold and reviewing a day's work done well. Some make bets on the hockey game that night.

OUR DAY IS DONE *The lights are out, except for the display windows and the big Kal Tire sign. Everything is cleaned and put away, fresh uniforms are ready. Out on the parking lot people call out to each other or give a wave before heading home. The next morning comes early.*

The staff turnover that occasionally caused Kal difficulties at the store level has been distinctly absent at the executive level. In fact, Kal Tire's management consistency may well be unmatched among companies of its size in Canadian business: in the company's entire history, every single senior partner it has ever had has remained on the job until retirement; not one has ever left to join another company.

That remarkable record is attributable to careful selection of individuals invited to join the team in the first place, and to their commitment once installed. But Kal also owes its rare qualities of reliability, innovation and equality to the corporate partnership management structure that has evolved from Tom Foord's personal values.

The majority of the partnership units is controlled by the Foord family. The balance is owned by Kal's working partners, all of whom are also senior management.

One of the biggest benefits of the system, says Ken Finch, is that it aligns management into a cohesive unit whose interests are focused on those of the company. "The corporate partnership creates a team based on working relationships, not unlike the ones we have in the stores," he says. "The fact that all senior managers are partners generates a sense of equality." He adds: "It reinforces our management style which is very much collaborative. No one person is smart enough to make all the decisions. In the end, we make lots of decisions that aren't unanimous, but we will definitely pay extra attention to the partner whose department or responsibilities are most directly affected by a particular discussion."

Indeed, the delicate dance with suppliers that John sometimes found himself enmeshed in hadn't much changed since the 1950s — except now Kal had become big enough to be both needed by and a threat to the tire companies. Pressure exerted on Kal by Michelin after the tire maker went into the retreading business was an example. For 40 years, Kal had been a franchisee of Bandag, a competing retreader. Michelin tried to leverage its position as Kal's supplier of truck tires to get Kal to convert to its retread process. In that instance, Kal stuck with Bandag, "but that decision had an impact on our tire business with Michelin on the truck side for a while," John says.

The use of pressure isn't all one-sided, he admits. But Kal's efforts to leverage its distribution channels to secure exclusive rights to a manufacturer's products are seldom successful. Tier-one suppliers such as Bridgestone or Michelin try to keep their supply lines as broad as possible. Still, the deal Kal has as sole distributor of Nokian winter and all-season tires in Canada is indicative of how good exclusivity can be: "Sales of Nokian products have gone from almost nothing to about one-third of our passenger and light truck business," John says.

Since taking over from Allan, John has overseen the consolidation of Kal's smaller warehouse operations into larger more centralized ones in Chilliwack, Edmonton, Brampton and Regina. "SKU [stock keeping unit] proliferation has meant we have to support a host of new wheel fitments and a range of tire sizes that has increased four-fold in 10 years," John notes. In Kal's business model, the warehouses are profit centres, like stores.

Though bigger, the new ones are more efficient and more easily managed, and hence more profitable. An investment in hand-held computers that scan bar-code labels on every product has facilitated tasks such as inventory, part picking and shipment tracking. "Since we can handle more volume more efficiently and more accurately, we can serve customers better," John says.

GOING INTERNATIONAL

By 2005, the Kal mining group that Archie Stroh began assembling in the 1970s to serve B.C. markets had expanded to the point that it accounted for a quarter of Kal's revenues. In Alberta, Kal Tire had 11 significant operations and more than 100 employees living in Fort McMurray to serve the oil sands. A chance conversation with a mining industry executive in 1996, however, piqued Archie's interest. "He wondered why Kal didn't have any operations in Chile," Archie recalls. "When I asked why we would, he said 'Because there are more mining trucks in Chile than all of Canada together.'"

After confirming the information, Archie and Ken Finch (and later the mining group's Joe Peshko and Flemming Sorensen) began making trips to South America to prospect for business. In 1997, Kal got its foot in the Chilean market with the purchase of a small section repair plant in Antofagasta, a port city north of Santiago that handled copper shipments from inland mines.

In 2007, Kal subsequently partnered with Carlos Grimaldi of Multillantas Grimaldi SA, a Mexican-based tire distributor, who also set up operations in Colombia, Mexico and Panama as Grimaldi-Kal Tire.

Chris Brothen, who had been with the organization for three years, was then asked to oversee Kal's Chilean business. Chris, who moved his family to Antofagasta, had to adjust to a business culture that frowned on a direct approach that was interpreted as aggressive.

When Tom showed up at meetings with suppliers, "he was always right on target and added a relevant historical perspective," says John Mullin.

"At first, I'd go to meetings, shake hands and ask for the order, which to them was an insult," he says. "You have to keep pushing, but you start to do it in a different way."

Kal had to show patience while acclimatizing itself in its first foreign venture. Its preferred management style is to give managers autonomy to make decisions affecting their areas. "We went out of our way to treat Chileans as part of our company," says Chris. "We tried to get them to establish goals, to look to the next horizon and chase those goals, but they kept looking to me, or someone who represented Kal Tire Canada, to make the ultimate decisions. These are well-educated, intelligent, logical businessmen. But for a long time they didn't feel they had the authority to make decisions." Ultimately, to get its point across, Kal promoted Carlos Zuniga, a Chilean who had been with Kal in Chile from the beginning, as general manager.

Kal's Chilean business was far removed from Alberta's oil sands. Its customers were mainly copper mines in the Atacama Desert, one of the driest places on earth. But Kal stuck to its business model; instead of simply selling tires, it sold its service as its added value. Rather than react to customers' tire problems, for example, it posted a full-time technician at mine sites and set up preventive programs that helped customers prolong tire life. The upshot was that both the miners and Kal's South American partner began to recognize the extra value created.

Although Chris began to appreciate the Chilean world the company was joining, it took persistence to convey Kal's culture to the locals. For one thing, there was Kal's absolute refusal to pay bribes, considered common in other countries in Latin America. And it took time to persuade South Americans that the AIMS, posted on office walls in Spanish, were a genuine standard that Kal adhered to. But gradually, each side came to see the other's point of view. "I came to an understanding of how the Latin culture works," says Chris, "and I was pleased that they've all eventually grabbed a bit of Kal Tire culture."

Kal's ethical approach proved a valuable asset when it added branches in other Chilean cities, building its local work force to 170. "People here know Kal Tire now," Chris Brothen says. "They know our colours, and they know our people. They know we pay our people on time, and we pay an appropriate wage. I walk into meetings and they say, 'Oh, you're with Kal Tire. Come on in!'"

Above, from left:
By 2007, Kal Tire had established a beachhead in Mexico through tire distributor Multillantas Grimaldi SA. Chris Brothen, Kal's mining man in Chile and Argentina.
Opposite, from top:
A Kal Tire/Grimaldi staffer checks tires in Mexico. To be in meetings sharing ideas with his father, Tom, is something Robert Foord treasures.

ROBERT FOORD
TAKES OVER MINING

Tom Foord had done all he could to kindle in his son Robert an interest in the business of tires. In the early 1960s, Tom and Jim Lochhead took him with them on a visit to the Lornex copper mine outside Kamloops. But while the world of giant trucks shod with two-storey-high tires had impressed the six-year-old, the tire business hadn't particularly. It wasn't until 23 years later, in 1987, that he fulfilled his father's hopes and joined Kal.

Robert spent the next 18 years in positions of increasing responsibility at Kal, justifying his father's faith that Kal was his destiny. By 2004, when Archie Stroh announced his retirement, Robert had already been a partner and vice-president of sales at Kal for seven years. It seemed a natural progression in 2005 that he should succeed his mentor, Archie Stroh, as senior vice-president and head of the mining group. Like Archie, Robert believed the potential of the mining division to export Kal's capabilities was limitless. And the performance of the South American operations had supported him.

Robert had seen enough of the global marketplace to understand that the mining industry's cyclical activity level depends on commodity prices. Shortly after becoming head of Kal's mining group he experienced the impact that the supply-and-demand pendulum could have on Kal. A dramatic spike in global demand for commodities triggered a surge in mining activity that led to a shortage of OTR tires. "Manufacturers couldn't make enough of them because they didn't make the investment in new capacity soon enough," says Robert.

Robert is grateful to have had the opportunity to work at Kal while his father was active in the company. "To be in meetings with him and share ideas is something I treasure," he says. "The past 10 years have allowed me to spend time with my father that I missed in the previous 40."

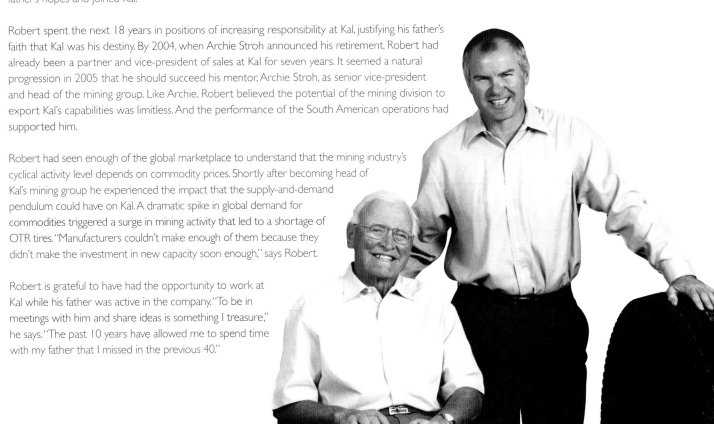

ADVENTURES
IN ARGENTINA

Kal's reputation inevitably attracted the attention of other foreign companies mining in South America. Barrick Gold, a Canadian company that is the world's biggest gold miner, contacted Chris Brothen when it needed tire specialists at a high-altitude mine it was developing just over the eastern Chilean border in Argentina. In order to get his Chilean staff to work as quickly as possible, Chris transported them to the mine, satisfied to accept Barrick's offer to deal with the stifling bureaucracy required to obtain Argentinian work visas.

Harsh didn't begin to describe working conditions at the mine site, at an altitude of 15,500 feet — almost three miles above sea level. "It's debilitating," says Chris. "You can't eat, because there's not enough oxygen to digest your food. For the first three days we lived on soup, and maybe a few crackers and lots of coffee because caffeine dilates your blood vessels so you can get more blood to your brain. In the middle of a meeting you'd nod off in mid-sentence." Mountain weather that featured savage lightning storms and near-hurricane-force winds didn't help matters.

Those impediments, though, almost paled in comparison to strangulation by South America's legendary red tape. Soon after returning to Chile, Chris learned that due to a foul-up concerning visas and registration of mining equipment that had come from Chile, the Argentinian police had jailed some of Kal's workers and impounded Kal's fully equipped service truck. To escape the predicament, Chris quickly created a new Argentinian company that would own the equipment and employ Kal's men. Although it took two days to make the arrangement, it wasn't the worst outcome. Kal Tire Argentina, the new entity, gave the Canadian company a solid platform from which to move into yet another South American country.

South America afforded Kal an opportunity to exploit its Canadian experience with OTR tires to offer superior service in the field. Aware that tires are miners' third biggest operating expense after labour and fuel, Kal showed customers how road maintenance and driver education could save them money. "If drivers go over rocks or drive too fast around corners, then everything we do to extend tire life is for naught," says Chris. "It's tough to keep the roads clear. But we emphasized that doing that, along with such things as monitoring air pressure and removing rocks from treads, add to the tires' service life."

A main thrust of Kal's customer education, says Chris, had always been to point out the cost if equipment is disabled due to lack of preventive maintenance. "When mining trucks hold 240 tons of coal worth $110 a ton, tire failure that causes the loss of a truck load becomes a costly proposition," he says. "Customers don't take long to understand that."

Above, from left:
Chris Brothen at the Veladero Mine in Argentina. George Frame and Robert Foord at the Ekati Mine in the Northwest Territories.
Opposite, from left:
Inspecting tires in Africa. Brenda Lyon at Mildred Lake, near Fort McMurray.

WIDENING
KAL'S WORLD

The worldwide commodity boom that fed the mining industry slowed significantly following a credit crunch and stock market collapse in the fall of 2008. Kal's strong balance sheet helped it weather the resulting business downturn.

In October 2009, Kal actually expanded its earthmover tire business with the acquisition of 51 percent of OTR Tires, a company based in Alfreton, in Great Britain's Midlands region. Though much smaller than Kal, OTR's history and business model were similar. Bob Skelton had founded the British company in 1977. His son, Chris, OTR's majority shareholder, remained with Kal as its managing director after the deal was completed.

The transaction represented Kal's ability to respond to changing business conditions in the OTR segment of its business. As mining companies around the world have consolidated to achieve the critical mass required to finance ever-bigger projects, they have increasingly outsourced functions demanding special expertise such as tire services. They prefer to deal with companies with a global presence to match their own.

Kal and OTR had already separately established their bona fides as capable global operators. For more than a decade, Kal had successfully exported the tire-service capabilities it developed in Canada. Since its 2007 partnership with Carlos Grimaldi of Multillantas Grimaldi SA, a Mexican tire dealer, it had added operations in Colombia, Panama and the Dominican Republic.

OTR Tires had exported its similar expertise to Africa, Western Australia and Norway. Bob Wallis, head of Kal's mining-tire group, was confident Kal could parlay its experience into more business. "At Kal we're used to operating in a very decentralized manner," he says. "We can use that skill to grow the mining group."

FORT MCMURRAY UPDATE

As promising as Kal's global mining-tire interests were, they still lagged the much bigger operation in Alberta's oil sands. In the late 1990s, while Kal's mining group was developing its new Chilean and Argentinian markets, complementary activity in Fort McMurray was growing.

The two theatres of action had a common link. As a manager of a Swedish-owned mine in Chile, Bob Bennett, a Canadian, had worked with Kal on one of its first South American service contracts. When he returned to Canada, Kal hired him to use his mining experience as Kal's area manager in Fort McMurray.

Bob immediately encountered the awkward economics of operating in a boom town. "There was a huge cost associated with doing business in Fort McMurray and we were selling ourselves short on our labour," he says. "We had to charge much more in Fort McMurray than our normal rates." Even paying higher rates didn't guarantee available workers; not everyone found Fort McMurray's frontier environment hospitable. For one thing, accommodation was prohibitively expensive.

Nor were customers forgiving in the quality of service they demanded. Kal Tire was more than ready to comply with the most rigourous safety standards; but it took a great deal of time and effort just to figure out how to do so with fewer resources than the operators had to create the regulations. "Our major employer had 5,000 employees, with a hundred of them in safety," says Bob. Bob was promoted to general manager of the mining tire group in 2004. Brenda Lyon, former credit manager in the Vernon office, agreed to take on the area manager's role in Fort McMurray.

As a mining man, Bob was used to the cyclical ups and downs of the industry. But he found the Athabasca oil sands region an anomaly; recessions appeared to have no impact on the area. "You just can't compare what goes on in Fort McMurray to any other area of business," he says. "The scale up there is so huge, it's hard to comprehend. And there was a lot of unchecked growth and cost overruns."

While some customers deferred spending in downturns, he says, they seemed to regard it as "catching their breath," a pause until markets stabilized. Meantime, Kal was under as much pressure as ever to add people and equipment in anticipation of any sign of a recovery. "We weren't laying anybody off," Bob says. "In fact we were hiring more people, buying more equipment and going full speed ahead to match the growth of our customers."

Opposite: Inspecting tires in Africa. **Above:** Inspecting a wheel assembly during a tire change-out.

THE "FAMILIES" BUSINESS

The perception that Kal is a family business is understandable. Immediate descendants and relatives of founder Tom Foord have played a part in the company's growth from its inception and continue to contribute to its success. For that matter, so does Tom, Kal's president for more than half a century, then chairman, and now founding chairman.

Yet "families" business would more accurately describe Kal. Every company has to refresh its workforce to accommodate retirements and growth. Recruiting from outside, as Kal did in the case of John Mullin and Mark Batchelor, for instance, can reinvigorate thinking by introducing new perspectives and ideas that succeeded elsewhere.

But Kal has always seen the benefit as well of hiring qualified relatives of existing employees. It would be foolish to overlook candidates raised on Kal's values and committed to maintaining them. And to Kal's good fortune, there has been a consistent supply of candidates who grew up hearing parents, grandparents or other relatives extol the merits of their career at Kal. A benefit of the phenomenon over the years has been the availability of new employees already acculturated to the Kal Tire way.

Michael Kinghorn, who succeeded his father Wayne, Kal's long-time advertising and marketing manager, exemplifies the phenomenon. In a previous position he had managed online marketing and databases for the Vancouver Canucks, handy skills as Kal developed its online presence. In addition to guiding Kal's online marketing strategies, he oversees Kal Tire News, or KTN, which features DVDs regularly distributed to Kal's stores. The DVDs include news and commentary and business updates, as well as addresses by senior management. Ken Finch comments that "the DVDs aren't intended to replace or have the same impact as a personal visit by a senior manager, but they're nonetheless a channel of communication."

RECESSION REDUX – CIRCA 2008

Although Kal managed to navigate past the worst of the 1981 recession, recognition of what could have happened had a sobering effect, jolting Kal out of complacency. At Tom Foord's insistence, Kal's young staff ferreted out waste and adopted strict cost-cutting. Measures taken to avert financial disaster were adopted as financial fundamentals, guiding Kal's operating style for years afterward.

Still, when the credit crunch in the fall of 2008 plunged the world into a recession, the average age of Kal's store managers was 35, too young to recall much of the downturn that had begun 25 years earlier in 1981. Ken Finch, though, had been part of the management that mitigated the damage in the early 1980s through cost-savings that kept Kal afloat and left it a leaner, nimbler company. Despite inevitable backsliding in the interim, "in 2008 we were a lot better prepared than in 1981. We knew what had to be done," he says.

Bob Wallis, then Kal's chief financial officer, bore much of the responsibility for identifying trimmable fat in 2008. He saw the credit crisis not just as a problem but also an opportunity to get the fiscal prudence program back on course. "All sorts of costs sneak in," he says. "It takes the harsh reality of a downturn to say, 'Let's address some things we should have taken care of long ago.'"

To deal with the credit crisis, Kal cut its capital expense budget by lowering the number of new stores from 20 or so over a five-year period to eight or ten — and specified that those would be in the West where Kal Tire's name recognition gained it the biggest bang for its money. At the same time, Kal shelved plans for a new office building in Vernon, cut travel and advertising, and eliminated social events with suppliers unless approved by partners.

Closer monitoring of operations led to adjustments as well. When diesel fuel price spiked, Kal cut deliveries from warehouses to stores to twice a week from three times. Full warehouses, though efficient when times were flush and stock turned over often, were costly when sales sagged and inventory sat on racks. So Kal pared inventory to free up capital that could be allocated more efficiently elsewhere.

Closer inspection of intra-company transactions also wrung inefficiency out of operations. When a store collects a commercial customer's tires for retreading and ships them to a Kal retreading plant, both the store and the plant take a specified profit on the service. "But we realized retread plants weren't passing nearly enough of the service cost on to the stores that handled transactions," Bob Wallis says. "And the stores, in turn, weren't passing enough on to their customers." Rather than raise prices and discourage customers, precisely when they didn't need a higher cost, Kal instead resorted to some creative thinking: the plants raised prices only to recover part of the operating expenses; for the rest, Kal solicited increased support from its loyal suppliers to help where they could.

Opposite, from top: In the retread process, pieces of under tread waiting to be applied to an OTR tire. Colin Foord, Kal Tire's longest-serving employee, also has a passion for his mom's Scottish roots.

My dad always made a point of going into the shop and talking to the guy who was changing tires. I try to do the same thing.

COLIN FOORD: KAL'S LONGEST-SERVING EMPLOYEE

Tom Foord's oldest son, Colin, loved working in the stores changing tires and doing service work. But as a single father, his first posting in 1972 to the Kal Tire outlet in Fort St. James (in northern B.C.) was problematic. At the time, there was little training for managers, so he was on his own running the business. And he had a two-year-old daughter, Mary, to care for.

Colin was determined not to let those obstacles stop him. Mary remembers being bundled up in the back seat of a service truck while her father handled a service call. She laughs that Foords seem to have tires in their blood: "To me tires still smell like home," she says.

From Fort St. James, Colin moved on to other Kal outlets, before deciding that what he enjoyed most was the equipment side of the business. When a back injury curtailed his ability to handle the physical aspects of the job, he took on the delivery of Kal's customized service vehicles from Vernon to the company's various outlets.

The job gives him an opportunity to meet store staffs across Canada and he manages to inject a Foord touch when he arrives at a Kal destination receiving the new vehicle. "My dad always made a point of going into the shop and talking to the guy who was changing tires," Colin says. "I try to do the same thing."

Colin is proud of the fact that, except for his father, he's the longest serving of Kal's employees. But when he retires, he'll leave behind a connection. Mary is married to Gerald Olstad, a Kal employee.

A memorable character, for instance, was the inept Kal store manager Sidney Sidewall, a.k.a. Joe Peshko, whose execrable work habits doomed him to failure until the Kal Tire way delivered him from his fate.

Above: Joe Peshko done up as the hilariously inept Sidney Sidewall, who could only be saved from his own bad habits by the Kal Tire way.

THE 2009 ANNUAL MEETING: KAL KEEPS A PROMISE

Kal first began holding annual meetings in Vernon the 1980s. The meetings — proudly organized internally without professional help — were conceived partly as a reward, partly as a training and information session, and partly to give employees from different areas an opportunity to meet and exchange ideas in a casual environment. Managers, assistants and associates freely mingled with shop workers and senior management, providing a fertile setting for a cultural exchange. From across the West, young men piled into busses bound for the Okanagan.

The meetings' business component often included the introduction of initiatives such as the 50/50 partnership and Team Share as well as training sessions. The business portion of the meeting eventually gave way to competitions ranging from basketball, bowling and beanbag tosses, to word games and a competition called Top Gun that pitted teams against each other to see who could change four tires the fastest.

A highlight for many attendees was the presentation of videos and skits prepared by senior managers that satirized Kal itself. A memorable character, for instance, was the inept Kal store manager Sidney Sidewall, a.k.a. Joe Peshko, whose execrable work habits doomed him to failure until the Kal Tire way delivered him from his fate.

Regrettably, the traditional annual meetings that contributed so greatly to Kal's spirit became a casualty of Kal's growth when it surpassed 2,000 employees. "It was part of our culture that we cared enough about our people to bring them in once a year," says Ken Finch, "but eventually we grew to the point where we just couldn't invite everybody." For a while, Kal tried alternating managers and salespeople one year and assistant managers the next. But it eventually outgrew even that format and was forced to hold annual meetings for only managers and salespeople. "It was far from ideal," Ken acknowledges. "But if we could connect with them once a year, it helped us build our culture across the company."

By far the biggest decision management had to make as the 2008 recession deepened throughout the fall was what to do about plans well under way for Kal's Annual Meeting in January 2009. Kal had arranged to fly managers, salespeople and their spouses — a total of 700 people — to Hawaii. The event was to be a celebration of Kal's 56th anniversary and a tribute to many who had been responsible for its success.

While gala annual meetings were probably endangered anyway due to Kal's growth, Ken Finch admits it especially made no financial sense to go forward with the 2009 meeting in Hawaii while Kal was otherwise engaged in as severe a belt-tightening exercise as it had ever undergone. "Cancelling it was a logical place to cut expenses when it became apparent that the economy wasn't going to turn around any time soon," he says.

In the end, though, management decided to carry on. Furthermore, the decision wasn't as difficult as it might have seemed to anyone who didn't understand Kal, Ken says. And it had little to do with possible cancellation fees or loss of hours of leadership training planned in conjunction with the meeting. Rather, it was concern for the emotions of employees if the long-anticipated trip were abandoned.

Avoiding that disappointment, in management's view, trumped any financial reservations. "Some of the wives had never been on an airplane," says Ken. "And most of those who had, had never been to Hawaii. The trip was as much to thank them as anybody else. It's the wives who have to put up with their husbands working all those long, long hours."

That the company would make the sacrifice in parlous times, of course, preserved the morale that Kal had spent more than half a century building. In fact, it significantly boosted it. Bob Wallis admits his job as chief cost-cutter wasn't made easier by the cost of flying employees and their spouses to Hawaii in the midst of a recession. "But that decision made me chest-thumpingly proud to be part of Kal Tire and of the people I work with," he says. "I can't think of another company anywhere that would have done that."

GETTING THE COST-CUTTING MESSAGE OUT

The Kal Tire News (KTN) video network, administered by Kal's manager of new media, Michael Kinghorn, demonstrated its value in November 2008. Two months after the credit crunch clobbered stock markets, panicked investors and began a world-wide recession, Michael produced a DVD and distributed it via KTN to inform Kal's more than 3,000 employees of measures being taken to weather the financial maelstrom. In contrast to the 1981 recession, KTN permitted Kal Tire to quickly communicate cost-cutting measures to more than 200 outlets and implement necessary adjustments that helped it weather the downturn.

Bob Wallis, Kal's chief financial officer, outlined economies management would be implementing, and reassured employees that "Our balance sheet is stronger now than it was two years ago." Some of the cuts being made, he candidly acknowledged, "are more symbolic than financial, but the purpose is to impress on every team member that cutting back during uncertain times is the right thing to do."

Managers from three B.C. outlets — Andrew Minchin of Nakusp, Dan Caterer of Merritt and Wes Ortwen of Princeton — reinforced Bob's message by maintaining their margins by boosting their sales effort, and by looking into such things as government wage subsidies for part-time employees.

Ken Finch, the final speaker on the KTN newscast, paraphrased philosopher Friedrich Nietzsche, noting that "What doesn't kill us, makes us stronger," to emphasize that smart managers learn from tough times to take better advantage in good ones.

Kal, he noted, is living proof of the truth of that message. It bounced back from the 1981 recession and it will do it again. "Our team will be the stronger for it."

By 2009 Tom Foord had been involved in the running of Kal Tire for nearly 60 years. That year the company reorganized management.

CHAPTER EIGHT: KEEPERS OF THE FLAME

> **Robert's kind of the keeper of the culture and that consistency in a company like ours is a huge strength.**

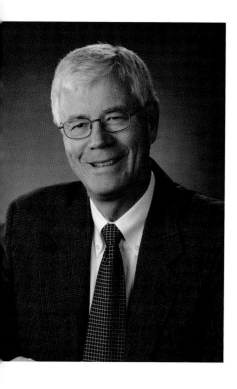

PASSING
THE TORCH

The 2009 Annual Meeting in Hawaii, the highlight of an otherwise recession-battered year, was a watershed for Kal. It employed 3,000 people worldwide; even if it only invited management representatives to a meeting, the logistics would be unwieldy — and likely become more impractical as the number of employees continued to rise.

Shortly after the 2009 annual meeting the company announced that Tom Foord would be moving from chairman to the newly created position of founding chairman. Ken Finch, 64 in 2009, replaced Tom, 87, as chairman. In turn Robert Foord, 51, would be succeeding Ken as president of Kal.

Management changes at Kal dating back to Tom Foord's buyout of Jim Lochhead in 1969 had historically been free of upheaval, unhappiness or resignations, and the 2009 realignment was no exception. The changes were designed to relieve Tom Foord from the chairman's duties that had expanded since the position had been created five years earlier.

In fact, the change of responsibilities wasn't all that great. For a year or so prior to becoming chairman, Ken had been fulfilling the chairman's role in addition to the president's when Tom wintered in California. "I told Tom that if I continue to do both jobs, I probably wouldn't have the energy to stay with Kal for more than three or four years," Ken says. "But if I resigned as president and became chairman the somewhat slower pace would allow me to stay a longer time, help out the management team and play a real role with Kal. Tom agreed that that was a good idea."

A logical succession plan made the transformation easier. Robert Foord had spent the last four of his 22 years at Kal as head of the mining group. Under his stewardship, the division's contribution had increased annually as a percentage of Kal's revenues. Robert succeeded Ken Finch, his brother-in-law, as Kal's president to lead the company in its next growth phase.

The changes naturally had the endorsement of senior management. "Robert's kind of the keeper of the culture and that consistency in a company like ours is a huge strength," says Bob Wallis. "It's not that the rest of us aren't committed to it, just that he's absolutely passionate about it, which is important in a president. He's a lot like his dad and Archie. He talks from the heart and cares about everybody. Tom and Archie and Robert all have that gift."

Robert, though conscious of having the Foord surname and its inherent cachet, has never flaunted it. Indeed, he's earned respect precisely because he refused to let a family connection weigh on decisions affecting his career. In Kal's structure, he points out, the president doesn't necessarily have moral authority over anybody else. "You may lead the team," he says, "but in the end, you're one more voice around the table. Dad never used his powers to push something the group wasn't in agreement about; neither did Ken and neither will I."

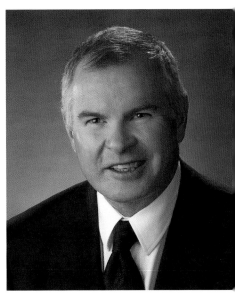

Bob Wallis, who had been chief financial officer and who had experience in various divisions of Kal, took on Robert's duties as head of the mining group. Ken Chaun, Ken Finch's son-in-law, was promoted to fill the spot Bob left as CFO, rounding out the management changes.

While only 33 when Kal hired him in 2003, Ken Chaun had earned solid financial credentials at the accounting and services firm KPMG and at Merrill Lynch, a brokerage firm. After the customary internship in Kal stores and a stint in its retread division, he put his accounting qualification to use succeeding Bob Wallis as vice-president of finance and chief financial officer.

A CFO'S APPRENTICESHIP

Ken Finch had an ally when he set out to persuade his son-in-law, Ken Chaun, that his future lay with Kal. Ken's daughter Lisa — Tom Foord's granddaughter and Robert Foord's niece — had grown up hearing her family expound Kal Tire's virtues. While earning her business degree at the University of British Columbia, Lisa had even done a project on a Kal retread plant, learning first-hand what her father had been talking about at home.

Her husband, Ken, had been ready to commit to learning the tire business from the bottom up. He found himself doing literally that after Kal posted him to a Vancouver store as part of its executives-in-training program. While lying under an RV, trying to screw a valve extension onto a rear wheel, Ken remembers feeling drips from a tank somewhere in the vehicle. "In that scenario, you ask yourself 'fresh water tank, gas tank or holding tank?'" Ken says. "I didn't like any of the possibilities."

The in-store executive internships aren't intended as initiation rituals, of course. But Ken felt co-workers would naturally be assessing his performance, just as they would each other's. "I'm sure they wondered how I was going to fit in," he says. "When they saw that I was ready to roll up my sleeves and get to work, I felt I was earning their respect."

His experience in the gravelly end of the tire business, Ken adds, put his new job into perspective. "When I saw what those guys could do — most of which I couldn't — they certainly had my respect," he says. "In the world of finance I was used to a small group of people working hard on a project for a few months, generating fees in the millions of dollars. Those guys were gunning wheels off a truck, getting out a bead axe and tire irons, repairing the tire and putting it back on — and making about $30."

From working in the Vancouver store, he then moved on to a retread plant. Within three years, the practical experience on top of his accounting and investment banking background qualified him to become a zone manager at 36 years old.

"Mr. April" 2001, Tom flexed his muscles in a charity "pin-up calendar" that helped raise money for Vernon's Hospice House.

"If I had not proven myself," Ken notes, "I never would have been respected as a manager by the men I was supervising who had 20 years of experience retreading tires. I knew all about spreadsheets and crunching numbers; they knew all about retreading tires," he says.

In 2008, five years after he joined Kal, Ken was appointed vice-president of finance under chief financial officer Bob Wallis. In 2009, when Bob took over Kal's mining group from Robert Foord, Ken, having completed his "apprenticeship," replaced Bob as chief financial officer. "But I still occasionally call the managers of the stores I worked with to find out how everybody's doing," he says. "Those guys taught me a lot."

Ken also emphasizes that nepotism is foreign to Kal. "The family was very careful not to pressure other family members to come into the business. They had to really want it. Robert Foord is one of the few who has seen and done it all. Anybody who has worked with him sees his appointment as a fantastic and natural thing. He has the passion and the skills, and a lot of the qualities of the man who got the whole thing started: Tom Foord."

KAL'S SECOND CHAIRMAN

Ken Finch, like Archie Stroh earlier, admits to having had to develop both a practical and philosophical response to the second thoughts he felt at leaving Kal's day-to-day operations. "After the changes were announced I sometimes thought to myself, 'Give your head a shake; why are you leaving? You love what you do,'" he says. "But eventually you have to do some things for yourself and for your family, because you never know how long life is going be."

With fewer responsibilities, and lower demand on his time as chairman than as president, a trip to Africa with his wife, Jean, in early 2010 topped his travel to-do list. He also intends to spend more time at his home on Lake Okanagan with his grandchildren. "I've only had four consecutive weeks off twice in my life," he says. "I'll be able to spend more time on the golf course, fly fishing and doing woodwork."

As Kal's chairman, he'll be a resource for senior management. He intends to continue speaking to Kal's management trainees, and will also represent Kal while speaking to outside groups. No longer as fearful of addressing groups as he once was, Ken speaks with a wry, quietly thoughtful style — and note-free when the topic is the source of Kal's success.

"I don't need notes when I'm telling anyone this stuff," he says, ticking off what he believes are the five points that have established Kal as a model business-school case study. Passion for exceeding customer expectations, and being driven by customer needs are fundamentals of the Kal Tire way, he says.

Kal's zone and senior zone management system, he maintains, has enabled the company to operate efficiently while keeping a decentralized management close to operations. "Kal's willingness to share profits through the 50/50 partnership, and its training and promoting from within, have

produced a great team," he says. "The culture of reinvesting profits and a patient, long-term approach that isn't driven by self-interest may have started out as a small-town approach, but we've proved that it works."

Certainly, as Kal appointed only its second chairman, it could point to tangible proof of success. In Canada, as of 2010 it boasted a network of 164 stores from Vancouver to Ontario, supported by 49 associate dealers who wear the Kal colours. Kal also served commercial customers with 10 retread plants and two OTR outlets, and ran four state-of-the-art distribution centres to manage its inventory of car, truck, industrial and earthmover tires. The 2009 partnership with U.K.-based OTR added 300 new employees, boosting the mining group alone to 800; by 2010, Kal's overall payroll was up to almost 4,000 in 17 countries.

Still, it wasn't the change that most impressed Bob Wallis, who'd been Kal's CFO for the decade-long growth spurt that had seen company sales surpass a billion dollars. Rather it was the consistency of vision. Tom Foord's simple observation — that the world runs on rubber — was just as valid when he joined in 2001, Bob says, and Archie Stroh and Ken Finch introduced him to Tom Foord.

"The whole thing started with Tom, and I was pretty impressed even then with what he'd created," says Bob, now vice-president of Kal's mining group. "Fifty-seven years later, there are differences in Kal's size, its products, where it operates and the tools we use to do the job. But Kal is still a Canadian-based, family company at its heart. I think that says something about the culture that Tom Foord built into Kal."

"Fifty-seven years later, there are differences in Kal's size, its products, where it operates and the tools we use to do the job. But Kal is still a Canadian-based, family company at its heart. I think that says something about the culture that Tom Foord built into Kal."

Echo Memoirs Ltd.
1616 West 3rd Avenue
Vancouver, BC
Canada V6J 1K2

WWW.ECHOMEMOIRS.COM
1 877 777 ECHO